Praise

'I've been a Professor o; _____ years, and I'm still over _____ ..i..ii i iiieei a new idea. This is not just a new idea. This is a great idea.'
— **Prof Marjan I Bojadjiev**, PhD, Provost of University American College, Skopje

'This is not just another sales book. This is the personal insight of a bold professional who provides his own experience, dilemmas and solutions, sometimes against dogmatic marketing paradigms. If you are a B2B consultant, this book is written just for you. Excellent book, modern topic, dynamic, educational, easy to read. Strongly recommended.'
— **Vlatko Danilov**, MSc, President of the Management Consulting Association

'Fantastic read! I caught myself taking screenshots of parts of the book, some of which focused on strategies that I couldn't wait to share with my partners. Other highlights were must-have how-to guides that are of tremendous help to my team.'
— **Borjan Sandrevski**, Co-Founder and COO at Fabricca

'Extremely useful and insightful book filled with plenty of real-life examples of how to acquire new clients for your digital marketing agency. I wish I'd had this book when we started our agency three years ago.'
— **Blagoj Gjelevski**, Co-Founder at Tivius Productions

'Dancho gives entrepreneurs and start-ups the arsenal to compete against the market leaders in the digital age. He provides actionable insight and a step-by-step guide to automating the sales process.'
— **Igor Madzov**, Programme Director and Co-Founder at Startup Macedonia

'This was an excellent read. Very few writers can simplify B2B lead generation – I loved it!'
— **Michael Adonteng**, Coaches & Mentors Unwrapped

'As I was reading the book, I realised that I need a dedicated employee in my law office that will focus on putting Dancho's steps into practice.'
— **Aleksov Dejan**, Owner of Aleksov

'Consultants always find it hard to market themselves. The ZZ approach, with its six-step model, simply put, should be an eye-opener to all. It was a great simple read while delivering a step-by-step guide. Thank you, Dancho.'
— **Reema Nasser**, Executive Director at The International Council of Management Consulting Institutes (ICMCI)

'GREAT book! I really love how the frameworks all fit together – I haven't seen that before and it's a great idea. I will wholeheartedly recommend Dancho's book to both my students and my fellow consultants. It's one of the best books I've read on marketing, and that says a lot.'
— **Joe O'Mahoney**, Professor of Consulting at Cardiff University

'The bible for digital sales outreach and how to get actual results.'
— **Martin Martinez**, Founder of MeetAlfred.com

'Wow! I am genuinely impressed with this outreach framework. Dancho managed to find the perfect balance between automation and manual nurture within the outreach process.'
— **Gerard Compte**, Founder of FindThatLead. com and Scrab.in

'Dancho does a great job of distilling great and necessary information for business leaders to succeed with their prospecting efforts. The beauty of this book is that Dancho is able to make his strategy and concepts easy to understand so that leaders cannot just read the book but use it as an action-oriented playbook.'
— **Gresham Harkless Jr**, Host of I am CEO podcast

SWEET LEADS

Harness the prospecting power of LinkedIn and Email to fill your calendar with qualified, high-value, B2B meetings

DANCHO DIMKOV

R^ethink

First published in Great Britain in 2021
by Rethink Press (www.rethinkpress.com)

Cover image © Shutterstock | Vector Image Plus

Illustrations by Martin Kovachki

Contents

Introduction

Everyone needs new clients, either to survive or to grow, and this is an ongoing need, not a one-time event. To get new clients, you need leads. The more, the better. And they need to be the right leads with the potential to turn into clients. Not the ones that waste your time and disappear, or were never going to be interested in what you had to offer, not a supplier or even a competitor.

Imagine if you could attract not just any new clients, but clients who are perfect for you and who make your work a dream, because you love working with them and they are over the moon at what you can do for them. Imagine if every lead you pursued had the strong chance of turning into such a client. Imagine every meeting you set up being with someone who is interested in hearing you out and with the likelihood that the meeting will turn into a sale. I can tell you that your ideal clients are waiting for you.

I embraced online outbound lead generation, or cold prospecting (you might also have heard it called social selling or outbound marketing), because I had to. In the first year of running my management consultancy, I needed to hire a team of ten people for a project that lasted two months. After that, I had no more work for them because there were no clients knocking on the door, but I did not want to let them go. To keep food on the table and my hive safe and intact, I had to step out of my comfort zone and reach out. Consultants don't like reaching out – they often think it damages their credibility. But now my core business is teaching others how to reach out to the right people, and that's what I offer you as you look for ways to take your business to the next level without the resources of a big corporation.

You're probably an SME or an eager start-up wondering how you can guarantee staying in business. The cold prospecting process works like this: you proactively search for leads or prospects who have the potential to be your ideal client, approach them through various channels (I will focus on LinkedIn and email in this book), build a relationship and move them towards a specific goal, in most cases a trial of your solution or a consultative meeting.

But let's take a step back. I know you picked up the book to help you find new clients, but first I'd like to introduce myself and what my friends the bees have to do with it all.

How I got here

I've been an entrepreneur since I was ten years old. I brought ten kilos of sweets back to Macedonia (my home country) from our family holiday in Bulgaria and bartered them for pens, rulers and pencil sharpeners. The classmate market was vast and I made the most of the opportunity. I was terrified when the teacher asked me to stay behind after school. What if my parents found out? Or worse, my grandparents. I would be grounded forever. But he only wanted to make sure I was doing fair deals (of course I was). Then he paid me the equivalent of a few euros (a lot of money to me then) to buy the rest of my stock of sweets for his grandchildren. That was when I first felt the buzz of making the right choice, doing a fair deal and getting something in return.

I carried on in high school when there was a craze for burning CDs in order to make the awesome mix that would win the girl of your dreams. You couldn't find a blank CD in any store in Kavadarci, my home town. So I made day trips to the capital on Saturdays and filled my backpack with 300 at a time.

I learned networking skills in nongovernmental organisations (NGOs) as a teenager, and I still think that is one of the greatest assets you can have in business. The friendships, acquaintances and relationships I formed back then made me a better person. And took me a step further than the majority of my peers.

When it was time for university, I thought of being a computer programmer like all my friends, but I was fascinated by business and still felt the spark I had experienced in childhood. Numbers didn't scare me; I find them comforting, knowing that if I listen to what the numbers say, I can rarely go wrong. So I chose to do an economics degree. At the same time, I sold Rakija (a type of grape brandy) from my home town (the best in the Balkans) and became a nightclub promoter – and managed to fit in some studying.

An assignment on mobile marketing gave me my next business idea. It was the mid-2000s, and nobody in the Balkans was attempting SMS marketing, so my three best friends and I started an SMS marketing agency.

The cherry on top was when we were selected as one of the World Bank global innovators for 2009. This brought me a lot of nerve-racking speaking opportunities in Brazil, India, Finland and the Balkans. I realised that to grow you have to step out of your comfort zone. In my final year of college, I was living my best life.

Then a respected friend from my NGO days recommended me to a Dutch development organisation to advise agricultural start-ups. I didn't know much about agriculture, but I come from seven generations of beekeepers. So I gained my first full-time job and a ton of responsibilities. In my three years there, I put four businesses on track.

Next came three years as head of R&D at the Macedonia office for a UK software and hardware company. I set up the Macedonia operation while learning about computer back end and programming. I was young and energetic, eager to learn and help. I freelanced as well, plus was studying for two masters degrees – an MBA and a separate masters in entrepreneurship.

I found myself juggling, hard. I was working four demanding jobs at the same time – a full-time job, a freelancing side job, and with two master theses on the way. It comes as no surprise that by the age of 24, I was burned out.

Nature always helps at these times, so I went for a walk in my family's bee field. If only I could be as productive as those bees, but also as free as they were.

Introducing the bees

I am a proud seventh-generation beekeeper and it feels like bees are part of our family. For centuries, beekeeping has been passed down the family, with the hope that my son will be the eighth generation. And yes, we do have family secrets on how to create a sweet honey.

Bees take no orders, but their lives are structured so that every bee is essential to the hive, and to the quality of the end product (our sweet honey). Bees are extremely intelligent, carrying out complex tasks and learning from their environment to gain rewards, but they are not selfish; they'll pass their skills on to other bees.

Their communication system is also highly advanced: they understand maths and physics, and know how to share their knowledge with the hive. They communicate through head-butting, jostling and dancing. If the bees are treated humanely, they stay with the hive by choice. And if they are not satisfied with their conditions, they leave. I was desperate to fly free of my job and start my own hive, to get back the joy of my ten-year-old self trading sweets. And, as luck would have it, my freelancing gigs boomed. I knew that it was the right time to make the move.

The next day, I was walking to my office feeling my usual Monday morning depression. You know that feeling? It's like your legs want to go home of their own accord. I spotted a bee buzzing happily in a purple flower as I walked into the building and that was the sign I needed. Within an hour, I quit my job. It wasn't perfect timing – I was getting married in four months, and we had taken out a loan to buy an apartment – but I learned from the bees, and so can you.

The founding of BizzBee Solutions

After our perfect wedding, my wife and I embraced the digital nomad lifestyle with our laptops in the back seat of the car. Every other week we were in a different European city, or we would choose to work on the beach for a couple of months. There was no more nine to five; we decided our own working hours. Then I got sick and we knew that to be financially stable in the future, we needed to set up a company – to expand our team. We wanted to start a family and be able to provide for them without worrying where the next gig would come from and whether we would be well enough to cover it.

Our first office was a rented apartment in an old building where you would smell cooking as you walked up the stairs. Every day, the scent of freshly cooked peppers, mixing with tomatoes, onions and sauerkraut, accompanied me as I climbed. Even though it felt like I could taste the neighbours' lunches, when I entered my fully equipped office for the first time, I could taste success. I saw the desks and computers ready for the four interns I had recruited. BizzBee Solutions – named after my friends, the bees – was real.

Within a year, I had thirty-two employees. We were working with entrepreneurs, helping them make the right business decisions. Back then, we had four main services – market research, business plans, product sourcing and lead generation. My favourite was, of course, lead generation. Outbound lead generation, to be precise. I had to master it in that first year to survive and save peoples' jobs, but it was also fun – a young industry with so much potential.

My management consultancy works primarily with consultants, software companies and agencies, because these are the people I can support the most. I help B2B start-ups and SMEs, which are under constant pressure to stay afloat. Start-ups and SMEs are leaner and more agile than corporations, and benefit from the secrets of cold prospecting. They are able to adjust their strategy when they've seen the previous week's reports, and try something new, test it and implement what is learned the next week. Using semiautomation can make the outreach process easy while maintaining a personal touch.

When my company embarked on cold prospecting, we found a lot of content but not much of practical help. One marketing guru advised taking between six and twelve months to set up a team and investing €300,000 to see results within two years. How many start-ups and SMEs have that budget and time?

I know you can get results in less than a year, investing around €50,000 and without spending anything on ads.

What to expect from this book

In this book, I provide a deeper understanding on how to make lead generation effective for your business, including a section on automation as a valuable tool.

I look at how to strategically use outreach for your business, including a tactical step-by-step guide on how to execute the outreach. Tapping into the wisdom of my friends the bees, I share my six-step framework for planning and executing a successful digital outreach campaign. This demonstrates how to set up your team to perform digital cold prospecting and control your lead generation, and how to predict and maximise the results:

1. Ideal Client Profile (ICP)

2. Database

3. Copy

4. Campaign execution

5. Nurture

6. Campaign optimisation

I called it the ZZ Framework. Unlike relying on marketing for leads, the ZZ Framework can target with 100% accuracy and enables you to approach only qualified leads who need your solution and are therefore highly likely to invest. You spend your time and energy on the potential clients who are most likely to employ your services.

This book is divided into two main sections, on planning and executing a successful outreach campaign. Section One, Digital Outreach Planning, covers the first part of the ZZ Framework:

- Defining your ideal client profile, commonly known as **ICP** (I call this 'flower scouting')

- Building a **database** of prospects that fit with you (collecting nectar)

- Creating **copy** for outreach (building honeycomb), mapping the timing and tone of messages as well as the content

Be prepared to spend lots of time on planning; my framework is thorough, and time spent in the early stages is time saved later.

Section Two, Digital Outreach Execution, features how to:

- Successfully **execute** an email and LinkedIn campaign (honey creation)

- **Nurture** your prospects (honey tasting)

- Track and **optimise** the results (refining the flavour of the honey)

There is a web page full of resources to support your outreach campaign at www.BizzBeeSolutions.com/ book-resources, which we regularly update with new tools, findings and templates. It also contains extra tables, exercises and case studies to supplement the ZZ Framework.

In reading this book, you will understand that human psychology is the same both online and offline, so your mindset and the principles you apply need to be the same. I will help you diagnose and cure digital outreach fever – when people behave differently in online communication compared to networking at a physical event, treating humans like statistics on a spreadsheet and wondering why this doesn't lead to fruitful connections. No matter how much automation you use, always behave and speak like a human being.

Dive in and follow the bees to find happy-ever-after relationships with your abundance of new clients.

Digital Outreach And The Marketing And Sales Synergy

It takes courage to embrace digital outreach. Seriously. Email marketing is forty years old and, of course, it has evolved, but digital outreach has acquired a negative image. When you say 'outbound email marketing', people think 'spam'. And it is true that some people do abuse the online world and automation to reach out to a larger audience. Send one million emails, and with a success rate of 0.002% you still have twenty clients. But you bother 99.998% (or 999,980 people) with irrelevant content. And email service providers put a lot of effort into stopping that.

Remember the term I introduced: 'digital outreach fever'? Let me give an example. If you go to a live networking event, you don't expect to talk to hundreds of people. You know that you won't make quality connections like that. You plan to talk to perhaps ten to twenty people, see if you are a good fit and, if so, exchange details and follow up after the event. If not, you simply excuse yourself and gracefully move on. Several fruitful conversations with potential prospects – which you can follow up with a call or a one-to-one meeting – makes a successful event.

The problem with email outreach is that those same people who understand the value of the human approach at physical events behave in completely the opposite way online. They are no longer interested in a good fit for their product, or fruitful conversations. They want to make hundreds of approaches, if not thousands – as many as possible, as automated as possible. Quantity over quality. And then they wonder why they can't connect with their cold prospects.

This is treating humans as numbers on a spreadsheet. Instead, it is essential to change the approach to thinking in terms of helping the target audience, rather than selling.

Yes, make use of automation. But don't put in the automation anything you wouldn't write manually. Understand the principles behind automation tools before you start using them.

In essence, automation takes a process that you do manually and repetitively, and uses technology to do it for you. So if you want to send fifty to a hundred emails per day, the automation system can do this for you – but with the same message.

The moment you start writing different automated messages (that make you sound like a robot), you are suffering from digital outreach fever. You are no longer trying to save time. I want to bring back the human-to-human approach in the digital world. We need to get back to basic communication, to when people used to talk to each other. Building a relationship is a long-term game, not a quick win.

In the high-ticket B2B world, the prices are high, the sales cycle is long and complex, and there are multiple stakeholders involved in the decision-making process. To proactively pursue high-quality prospects, building relationships is the **only way** to turn those prospects into clients.

When prospects come to you (inbound leads), they are aware that they have a problem and are actively looking for a solution (problem-aware, solution-aware). If you reach out to potential prospects, some may not (yet) know that they have a problem, so are not ready to look to you for a solution. Approaching people (outbound leads) requires nurturing, until they recognise the problem and are ready to move towards a solution.

This means that some companies you reach out to will be quickly disqualified (ie clearly not viable prospects). However, with others you gain credibility when you open their eyes to the awareness that things can be better. Having established a relationship makes it more likely that, with the realisation that they have a problem, it will be you that they reach out to for the solution.

I will show you how to build these relationships through effective digital outreach, but before we dive in, we need to establish some ground rules. You have probably tried a lot of marketing and sales approaches that provided results to some extent. However, only large companies can afford large marketing and sales teams that integrate marketing and sales.

How about small businesses? I was a one-man band for several years, doing everything myself. When we were big enough to have an operations team, I focused on the marketing and sales functions. From there we built a small marketing and sales team but our resources were still limited so we had to get creative, measure, adjust and be agile.

SMEs can't afford a lot of marketing and salespeople, and must choose the right balance. The two disciplines sound like different approaches. Marketing people argue that a successful business needs content: ads, funnels, email marketing, newsletters, brand awareness, thought leadership, social proof. Their mantra is: 'Our content attracts prospects and moves them towards closure, so you don't need to put extra work into sales.'

On the other hand, the sales team who are responsible for their own lead generation (not those who depend on marketing for leads), will argue: 'You don't need marketing, as we can find, approach, build relationships with and close clients.'

Who is right? Depending on the industry specifics, and the type of business, you could probably find success with 100% marketing or 100% sales. But it's not like SMEs have extra cash to throw around. Rather, they see the value in both approaches, when used properly, as well as the synergy between them.

Let's look at each of them separately.

100% marketing

As a marketing team, your job is to cast a wide net and bring in potential clients. Once you know your ideal target (your ideal client profile – ICP), the goal is to create as much content (text, audio and video) as possible to attract the ideal client. But you don't know who is consuming that content. It could be someone who just wants to learn, a competitor or someone else who does not match your ideal criteria (maybe they don't need what you are selling or don't have the money, for example).

On the positive side, there are marketing concepts that could bring you great results. Here is the typical 100% marketing concept and how it works.

MARKETING-DRIVEN SALES

Generate traffic

Front-end funnel

Email campaign (SOS) → Nurture (Newsletter)

Deliver a webinar

New client

Here's the concept in more detail:

Generate traffic

Traffic can come from paid ads, content (blog, podcast, video), SEO, organic traffic, Quora, HERO (a platform called Help a Reporter Out), freelance platforms, social media posting, social media networking on various groups, etc. Of course, there are more advanced traffic techniques (creating web summits, online magazines, physical events, challenges, affiliate and other more complex events) but these are not often used in the SME world. However the traffic is generated, the end goal is to bring it to your front-end funnel.

Front-end funnel

This is usually a simple web page where the visitor leaves their email address and gets something in return. Regardless of where the prospects come from, your goal is for them to subscribe to your newsletter or give their email in order to download an e-book or video, for example. But the end game is to capture their email, Facebook account or any other channel that you can use for follow-up marketing. You capture your traffic by providing something for free, or cheaply.

Self-liquidating offer

A more advanced front-end funnel in which you charge a small amount (usually in the €10 range) to ensure there is a commitment: the prospect is not just interested in free stuff. You can invest some budget in advertising, and if enough people spend the small amount you break even. You are left with leads, which didn't cost you anything, that you can use to upsell to more expensive solutions.

Email campaign SOS

The Soap Opera Sequence was popularised by Russell Brunson in his book *DotCom Secrets*.[1] It's a series of five email messages sent over five days to trigger specific reactions in your prospect, with the goal of getting them to respond and move down the funnel.

Newsletter

The SOS sequence can have between 5% and 20% success rate: over the five days, between 5% and 20% of people who subscribed to the mailing list or paid for the front-end funnel offer will proceed towards the next step (the webinar). But that means that the rest, 80–95%, will not. And it is a pity to lose them. Perhaps they are not ready to buy and they need time. A newsletter keeps your business in their mind as a potential supplier for when they need your solution.

Deliver a webinar

The webinar is expected to be delivered live by an experienced salesperson or the founder/CEO. A recording of the webinar can be replayed to anyone who requests it. This way the key presenter only has to be available once.

---

1   R Brunson *DotCom Secrets* (Hay House Business, 2020)

New client

Three-quarters of the purpose of the webinar is to establish rapport and provide value and only the last quarter is to actually sell your services. As the attendees are marketing leads (without any manual pre-qualification), there could be a lot of participants. However, what is important is the conversion percentage – how many pay for the promoted solution.

So, 100% marketing does have its uses, and I know a lot of companies that rely on it. We use the marketing system in BizzBee Solutions. We give e-books and digital assets for free, in exchange for an email address. Once we have someone's email, we have an SOS email sequence, followed by a fortnightly newsletter.

A lot of widely recognised brands can afford to rely solely on marketing. Look at Russell Brunson, for example. He's built an empire based on his marketing strategies, and we can't deny that they work. He's using each and every way of marketing not only to gain more traffic but to close more customers.[2]

If you are in his target audience, you'll get targeted by the usual Facebook ad. It won't lead you to his most recognisable and profitable product, ClickFunnels, however. No. You'll land on one of his book pages. There you'll be met with an offer that is hard to refuse. If you cover the shipping costs for the book,

---

2   Russell Brunson, www.russellbrunson.com/hi

you'll get the book for free. There will be some other sales opportunities on the page as well, each leading to a well-thought-out and ethical offer in exchange for your email address. And then the saga begins. You're his subscriber and end up in his whirlpool of well-designed marketing. Free courses, free webinars, free templates – each with its own urgency and scarcity. Each offers immense value for free, but you just need to buy one thing to make good use of his knowledge. Guess what? His SaaS (software-as-a-service) – Click-Funnels. And it works for him quite well.

Brunson and his team will never pitch you this software one-to-one. His sales team only sells services starting at a couple of thousand dollars. And this is where the following question pops up: is the 100% marketing concept only suitable for cheaper solutions?

There are advantages to the marketing concept. It is an automated process, bringing cold prospects directly to your webinar and turning them into your clients. The front-end funnel is usually free, or low value, and then your prospects are pushed up the value ladder to a more expensive solution. If they are happy, sales can pick them up, and offer them even more expensive solutions. Low-priced offers cover the cost of getting leads that can be followed up with other offers. The webinar can be automated, or, even if it isn't, you can present to a large audience rather than multiple one-on-one meetings.

The main disadvantage is that it is fishing with a net, and will catch a lot of irrelevant leads. Also, any marketing that collects traffic requires ads (Facebook ads, LinkedIn ads, Google ads, YouTube ads, site-specific ads), so needs a marketing budget.

Another concern is that a strategy like this only works for cheaper or entry-level solutions. Nobody buys an expensive service just from seeing a Facebook ad. You can raise awareness and bring prospects to lower-value products, but rarely can you push them to buy an expensive solution through marketing alone. For that you need a salesperson who can get the client on a one-to-one call and discuss their problem and potential solution. People require the human touch.

100% sales

I have discussed how B2B marketing can exist without sales; can B2B sales exist without marketing? I believe it can, to some degree.

The B2B sales process is probably familiar. You build a database of prospects, qualify them (ie make sure they're appropriate), reach out to them via different channels and move them towards a meeting that ultimately converts them into clients in a process that looks like this:

SALES-DRIVEN SALES

Build a database

Qualify prospects

Cold prospecting

Schedule a meeting

New client

- **Build a database:** The sales development representative (SDR) or business development representative (BDR) builds the database manually, so it contains only highly targeted leads. A typical database will include company information, a relevant position within the company and their contact information. People change jobs frequently so the database needs to be frequently validated, updated and enriched to be useful.

- **Qualify prospects:** Once the database is built, you need to qualify the prospects based on criteria relevant for your business. Although some companies can match the firmographics (company profiles: geography, size, industry, etc) or even have the right person within the company, they could still not be a good fit. It is better to disqualify companies at this stage, rather than spend effort on later steps only to come to the conclusion that they are not relevant to you.

- **Cold prospecting:** The salesperson approaches the prospects using a mixture of cold calls and cold emails to see if there is any interest. They usually try three or four times before giving up. Some prospects will not answer; others will respond negatively – but some will respond positively. LinkedIn is also a great outreach channel.

- **Schedule a meeting:** This is where the salesperson can present your solution, explain what kind of problems you solve and show testimonials or case studies.

- **New client:** If the prospect is satisfied with the presentation, and believes you can help, they will eventually become a client.

So, sales can actually work without marketing. A qualified database leads to proper outreach, which leads to a meeting, which leads to a client.

The main advantage with the sales approach is that you are always working with highly targeted prospects who you know are relevant and potential buyers. You are proactively approaching relevant leads, not waiting for them to come to you. You know how many leads you can approach daily / weekly / monthly and can estimate the results.

The main disadvantage is that building a database, reaching out to prospects and nurturing them until they are ready is costly, time-consuming and labour-intensive. You need a whole team to work on the entire process.

Relying only on sales via freelancing platforms in the early days of my current business was one of my biggest mistakes. But it can feel logical at the beginning of your entrepreneurial journey. Marketing sounds expensive and to be avoided if you don't have the budget.

In an ideal world, I believe that effective outbound prospecting is the backbone of a business, ensuring an inflow of new clients in a predictable, systematic way. But a company cannot be purely outbound-orientated. It still needs to create some content for marketing purposes, and for building thought leadership and credibility. The sales process is far easier if you have strong marketing assets (e-books, white papers, reports, case studies, etc). It is easier to convince a cold prospect if you can show evidence of how you've helped a similar business.

The point is that you still depend on marketing, for although you have control over the entire sales cycle, the prospect will want to check you out: they will want to look at your website, your blogs, your authority on the topic, your social proof. If the prospect is not convinced of your authority, you will lose them. The point of marketing is to ensure that if the prospect tries to research the business, they will be excited. This is where marketing can support your sale.

The ZZ Framework

If sales-only and marketing-only concepts work, why should we invest in both marketing and sales then? First of all, they are there to support each other. You don't need to invest heavily in marketing activities, such as spending thousands of euros on paid ads, just so someone can download your e-book. Nor should you rely solely on sales and hope that your credibility will speak for itself and that clients will simply take your word for it.

We tried both approaches in my company. A lot. It all comes down to the industry you operate in, the business model, your business and your client preferences.

Because we provide a high-ticket B2B service, we've achieved far better results with cold prospecting, properly carried out. We work with agencies (real estate, marketing agencies, sales agencies, software development), consultants (management consultants, digital transformation consultants, leadership consultants, negotiation consultants, etc) and enterprise software providers. Synergy is key. And BizzBee's 400-plus clients prove that we've found the perfect balance between marketing and sales.

The ZZ Framework aims to help SMEs achieve synergy between marketing and sales, however limited their resources, by making use of technology and automation. It is designed to adapt the sales approach for SMEs, while supporting the sales process with automation and marketing.

Along the way, we made mistakes and learned from them, and upgraded our processes every time. The six-step ZZ Framework is the result of our experience.

Before we dive into Section One, Digital Outreach Planning, take a good look at the ZZ Framework. It's the visual representation of this book's core.

THE ZZ FRAMEWORK

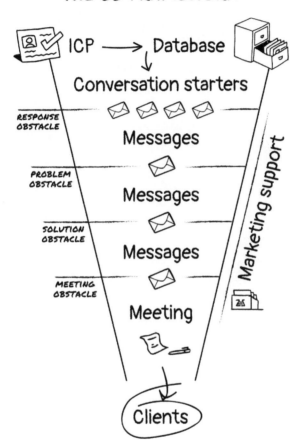

SECTION ONE
DIGITAL OUTREACH PLANNING

1
Ideal Client Profile (Flower Scouting)

The Ideal Client Profile Framework

To make sweet honey, the bees have to get the first step right – finding the flowers where they can collect the best nectar. How do they decide?

For starters, they are drawn by the flowers' physical characteristics: their bright colours and the shapes and patterns on the petals. And their fragrance: the aromatic promise of sweet nectar. But researchers have found that the attraction goes beyond what the eye can see. There is also electricity in the air.

As bees fly through the air, they typically end up with a positive charge. Flowers, on the other hand, tend to have a negative charge, at least on a sunny day.

When a positively charged bee arrives at a negatively charged flower, it finds pollen.

Although bees have tiny brains, they are swift learners. If they repeatedly visit an empty flower, they will quickly abandon the entire patch, and tell all their hive-mates to do the same; the whole colony will seek fresh pastures.

Bees also look for nectar with a high sugar content, because that means they have to do less work to make their honey. Nectar with lower sugar content contains more water, and the bees make the water evaporate by fluttering their wings; it literally costs them physical effort if they start with lower-quality nectar.

I'm sure you can already tell how to apply this to business growth. If you want the results of your outreach to taste honey-sweet, you need to start with the right flowers. Or, in business terms, the right prospects. The prospects' quality (likelihood of turning into clients) can vary immensely, so how can you possibly know which flower patch of prospects to visit? The answer is in defining your ideal client profile (ICP).

Figuring out your ICP from the start can save you a lot of marketing and sales effort. It's like the bees and their easy-win, top-quality, high-sugar nectar.

For a B2B company, an ICP is a hypothetical business or organisation that would get the most out of the solution the company offers. Defining who would get the *most* benefit is where the challenge lies. Your effort, energy and money shouldn't be invested in each and every client group that might benefit from the solution you provide. You need to find the top three client profiles for whom you can provide the most value and that are most likely to become clients quickly.

My company, BizzBee Solutions, has worked with over 400 entrepreneurs, start-ups and SMEs. We've talked to their founders, CEOs and directors to build up a picture of what helps them grow their businesses. In this chapter, I will outline what we've learned about what works and what doesn't in B2B ICP identification. And let me tell you the importance of knowing your ICP.

We worked for one of the biggest payday loan providers in Bulgaria. Since inception they had collected more than €250 million and granted loans of €200+ million, in five countries. All this was done with a relatively small team of 130 employees. They were ready for the next level.

When they approached me, they needed help to decide on the next country to expand into. The choice was between Poland and Colombia. One is a European country (with all the advantages and disadvantages), while the other is in Latin America (far away from their previous business). Their ICP research explored both countries, the nonbanking industry and market, and the fast loans segment in which they were operating. Even though initially we had more confidence in the Polish market (mainly because of the cultural similarities), our ICP research showed that the Colombian market was the place to be. The payday loans that the Latin American market offered were there for the taking. The results from our research surprised them and made them rethink their entire strategy.

Knowing your ICP won't help you if you don't change anything in your business as a result. On the other hand, once you do know your ICP you can:

- Enrich your solution (product, service, software) to address your potential clients' unique problems.

  In my own company's experience, most of our solutions are developed in direct response to feedback from our ICPs. We know who we want to work with and we actively listen to them. The upsells we develop emerge so naturally that we don't even need to try hard to sell them.

- Tailor all your marketing efforts – both inbound and outbound – to the same ICP, meaning that the copy for your website, emails and social media all talks to the same target person.

- Tailor your sales efforts to the ICP's needs. Only then can you experience the full benefit of properly defining your ICP.

I once had a call with an SME from the US. They wanted to target the EU market for their visual content management system (CMS). They knew what kind of businesses they wanted to target, and which positions to approach, and now they needed our help in lead generation.

We did our homework, and during the second call, I started asking questions specific to the EU market – which, surprisingly, they didn't know much about. They assumed that what worked in the US, where they were successful, could be replicated in the EU, and were surprised when we explained the differences in the market. For example, there were completely different supply chains in the EU.

We took a step back, and instigated a proper ideal client identification. The insights from the process helped the client to tailor their marketing and sales effort to the EU market. They couldn't expand into the EU until they had completed work on their ICP.

To summarise, a well-defined ICP can make or break your business – especially if you are a small business, and don't have the budget to experiment until you figure it out.

At BizzBee Solutions, we've created a framework – the B2B Flower Scouting Framework for ICP-defining, named thanks to the bees' inspiration – to help SMEs and high-ticket service providers define their ICP. This is the framework you're about to work through.

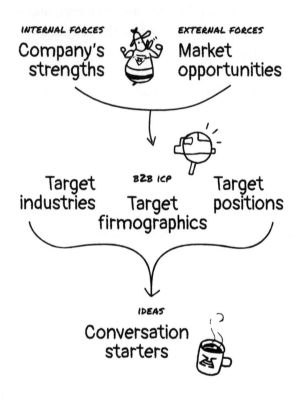

FLOWER SCOUTING FRAMEWORK
FOR ICP-DEFINING

INTERNAL FORCES
Company's strengths

EXTERNAL FORCES
Market opportunities

Target industries

B2B ICP
Target firmographics

Target positions

IDEAS
Conversation starters

In B2B, defining your ICP is a complex task. You need the right industry, firmographics (company profiles) and people all in place to have a successful outreach. This chapter will take you through the required steps:

1. **Internal forces:** Although a lot of business theory suggests starting from the market, I would argue that you need to start from your existing

business: understand the nature of your business, the benefits you provide and who your existing clients are. Then reflect on who you want to serve.

2. **External forces:** Once you know your business's strengths, you can look at the type of companies that could benefit the most from your offering – and your competitors' clients.

3. **Define the ideal client industry:** Understand the industry you are targeting. Is it growing or shrinking? Which industries can you explore on LinkedIn? Based on your strengths and the market opportunities, you can create a preliminary list of industries that have the potential to be your ICP.

4. **Define your ideal client firmographics:** These are characteristics that your target companies share that you need to understand to refine your ICP (company size, location, subindustry, etc).

5. **Define the ideal positions:** Once you know your ICP you can look at your target companies' organisational charts and find the people who are most likely to be interested in your offer – their official job titles, responsibilities, position variations, etc. These are your prospects.

6. **Conversation starters:** You also need to understand what kind of pain or problems your prospects have, both industry-specific and position-specific, that are relevant to

your business. These insights will shape your marketing strategy.

Internal forces

If you are starting a new business, the usual advice is that you need to look at the market opportunities, find a niche, build a solution for that particular niche and then just sell it to them. This is indeed the right way to launch a new product or service and it is highly recommended for everyone who is starting something new. It's good to be an entrepreneur.

But your company has already been in business for a while and you already have a solution. You already have clients who appreciate what you provide and you are generating revenue to some degree (hopefully, to cover your costs and some extra) – so it makes no sense to start from the market.

Strangely, most consultants helping companies build their ICP ask them to start from scratch, disregarding their established business and clients. Which is quite weird.

A software development cycle can take six to twelve months, or even longer, to get to a minimum viable product (MVP). Service providers require a similar amount of time to create a good service. So should you just disregard what you have created? Not a chance!

Isn't it better to look at your strengths and search for clients accordingly? And incorporate what you've learned so far?

I believe in strengths. That is how businesses are founded. As a serial entrepreneur, I tried several businesses, but I found my passion in B2B sales. I know that some people find the B2B sales cycle boring, hard and less attractive than B2C. Not me. A complex B2B sales process, with multiple parties involved and a longer sales cycle, means that you need to make extra effort and focus on relationship-building. I love doing this, so it was an easy choice to build my business around it.

I would rather consider my strengths and my existing products and services, and look for market opportunities that I can explore with my existing (or slightly tweaked) attributes, rather than starting with the latest market trend that would require me to be someone else. If you look at the nature of your business, the benefits of your solution and the existing or previous clients you've served, these three aspects will be at the centre of better understanding your ICP.

What is your business type?

By now you'll understand that a one-solution-fits-all approach does not work. I used to find it so frustrating that I could find a perfect solution for one client, but when I tried it for the next client, it just collapsed.

41

This got me thinking: why do some clients get fantastic results but others don't? Is it down to luck, or is there a data-driven pattern that we can depend on?

Not all companies are the same. We should not treat them as though they are. We worked out that there is a pattern in the 400-plus B2B companies we have worked with, and created a framework around that pattern. All B2B companies fit into one of the four quadrants in the table below. The sooner you know which quadrant your business is in, the faster you can apply the tailored solutions.

TYPE OF BUSINESS

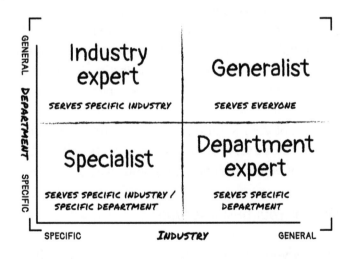

1. Generalist

These businesses offer quite a broad and general solution. It can help any business and any employee, whatever the industry they work in and at whatever level. As such, they have a broad spectrum of experience, but can lack specialisation.

In my opinion, most businesses are generalists. This category includes many consulting companies, web design/development companies, mobile app development companies and marketing agencies. Their services can be used almost by any company, in any industry.

A generalist has a broad B2B audience – which is a good thing. A common question that I am asked is, 'Why would you focus on one target when you could serve everyone?' However, it is necessary to define the ICP and create separate marketing and sales strategies for each target.

How can a generalist SME reach out to a larger audience? The only way is to focus the marketing effort one segment at a time. Let me ask you this – if you had a limited marketing budget of €1,000, who would you approach? When working with limited resources, you must focus on the people who are most likely to buy. That is the core of the ICP concept.

2. Department expert

This business can help any type of business, but the solution is department-specific. It has some degree of specialisation, but it is not industry-related. For example, CRM software like HubSpot targets marketing and sales people across any industry. Accounting software QuickBooks and Xero target the financial and accounting departments across industries worldwide.

When you know which department team you are talking to – sales, HR or financial teams, for example – you can tailor the conversation to those people.

I have worked with a lot of clients in this bracket: HR software providers, mindset coaches, financial options coaches, negotiations consultants and many more. They have strong expertise in their field that can be applied across a range of industries. They need an ICP to better understand who they serve. But having a cross-industry focus makes it hard for department experts to fully understand the client need.

3. Industry expert

These businesses serve companies only in one specific industry, and provide significant value to that industry. Many generalists evolve into industry experts, specialising in one or more industries – for example, agriculture consultants, logistics coaches, healthcare web development companies, FinTech (tech companies specialising in the financial industry) and MedTech (tech companies specialising in the medical industry).

I've worked with a few companies that are industry experts – for example, a client from the US offering a medical AI (artificial intelligence) solution for doctors, agencies specialising in marketing for services to ecommerce or retail.

If your expertise is industry-specific, you have a deep understanding of the problems that particular industry faces and what your target needs. But this industry focus usually lacks the specific department needs. Think about how you can provide a department-specific approach for an existing industry.

4. Specialist

This business has a solution for a specific industry that solves a specific departmental problem. A specialist can have a huge number of potential prospects – millions; it just needs to be quite specific.

A good example here is HR software for the auto industry, or marketing consulting for agriculture businesses. In a B2B business model, the more focused the niche the better. It may sound counterintuitive at first. How can reaching fewer businesses be a good thing? Think of it this way: the more specific your focus, the more specialised your company becomes. Large companies love to work with companies that have certain specialisations.

I was working with a Norwegian company that focused on manufacturing companies that need help printing marketing materials internationally for exhibitions and shows. Quite a specific niche. And within twelve months of working with us, they got €30 million in funding.

Where are you on this grid? It is much easier for niche companies to define their ICP, because they have already defined their target up to a point. If you are in the generalist axis, you need to spend quality time on identifying your ideal target profile.

Knowing this, the next step is to look at your strengths – your existing products and services.

Benefits vs features

When looking at your business strengths, don't focus solely on what you do – the services you provide or the features of your software. Knowing how your clients *benefit* from your solution can give you a different perspective on your ICP.

'Solution' is a general term, intended to include all products, all services, the mix of both, and any complex offering that could be set up. And you need to take a better look at yours, through the benefits prism. The key question is – which problems are you solving with your solution, and for whom?

I've seen plenty of software companies, for example, that are so focused on the functionality, features and case studies that they forget to tell a potential subscriber how they will benefit from using the software.

Other companies do understand the value of benefits over features, of course. I was working on market research for a software company that had developed meeting management software (MMS). They could have focused on all the functionality that their software shared with any other MMS – collaboration, security, document sharing, recording, voting, etc. Instead, we looked at the core benefits their solution offered. We then looked at the market and identified which segments most appreciated the benefits their solution provided. Surprisingly, we determined that it was company board members who saw the biggest benefit in the solution. Based on this ICP research, the software company focused on board members and added more functionalities that better served this specific target market.

The process for defining the benefits you provide is quite simple. First, list all the features (facts about your solution) that you are proud of. Focus on features that make you stand out from your competitors and make your solution unique. Don't go into too much detail. A few key features are enough to add credibility; if you have too many, you might get lost in the process.

For software companies, your features can be functionalities that you have implemented. I know you will be good at listing all the features of your software, because I hear this quite often: My software can... [feel free to finish the sentence].

For consultants, your features might be a process you follow, a framework that you apply or your input into the work. A certification, MBA or PhD adds to your credibility as a consultant, so these are all features.

Second, you need to convert these features into benefits. What is your client trying to achieve by using these features? How does each feature give clients a reason to buy? List the top five benefits that represent the core of your solution. These are your strengths, and you definitely want to choose your ICP based on them.

If you are a software company, think about how clients will use your features and what they are trying to achieve, or what kind of problem they are trying to solve. This should also be the key focus for consultants. What particular result does your client want to happen? That is your benefit, not the fact that you use Business Model Canvas, Porter's Five Forces or needs assessment.

Third, once you know your benefits, start proactively looking at the market, identifying new segments that need the same benefit – segments that you've never considered before. In many cases, these niche segments are also neglected by your competitors.

What type of clients have you served so far?

Take out your list of current and previous clients. They also give an insight into your business and your strengths.

CHOOSING AN IDEAL TARGET
BASED ON EXISTING CLIENTS

I have worked with several entrepreneurs who started off with a clear perspective on who their ideal client was and spent a lot of energy and resources building a solution that targeted that audience. And then they realised that they didn't really want to work with those clients: they are hard to sell to, difficult to work with or a huge energy drain. In the 'ideal' world of your ICP, you can choose who you want to work with, so choose wisely.

If you reflect on your current client portfolio, I am sure there will be some clients that were not as happy as they should be. They were expecting more, wanted to pay less or simply did not get what they expected from your solution. Meanwhile, other clients jumped for joy at the value you added. Which clients really appreciate what you deliver? This will help you understand who can benefit from your solution the most.

I started my consultancy by coaching solo entrepreneurs who were planning to start businesses. I tend to give my all, invest myself in everything that I do. I got involved in clients' market research, every business plan, every meeting and every conversation. I found it frustrating that I rarely got a call from a former client who had indeed started a business. No matter how much coaching you give someone whose business is still an idea, there is a lot you can't control about their success. I yearned to feel not only valued and appreciated, but useful. I wanted to help people succeed, not just to put thought and hard work into an idea that sounded great on paper but was never seen again.

I realised that to change my working life I didn't need to change myself; I needed to change the people

I worked with – my target. Rather than people who have ideas, I needed to work with those who could carry out their ideas, who didn't stop at the first obstacle, who weren't afraid to take action and push things further. I was an entrepreneur once, too. Nearly every business owner starts as one. Some of my best and most appreciated clients were entrepreneurs.

The thing is, they have so much on their plate. The entrepreneur's world is like a whirlpool of problems and challenges that need to be faced: finance issues, market issues, legal issues, accounting issues, you name it. For me, the energy it takes to solve all these problems wasn't worth it. Especially when entrepreneurs can so easily quit and jump on to the next best thing. Their next entrepreneurial adventure.

As my company progressed into an SME, I realised that the SME world is entirely different. You generally have all these types of issues sorted already and focus solely on growth. And that's what I wanted and still crave to do – help companies grow. I shifted my company's focus, from entrepreneurs to SMEs, and asked myself what I could do for them, how I could provide value.

The main reason why you should look at your existing client base is that these people have actually paid for your solution. I've heard so many frustrated owners claiming that their family and friends were so excited about their new business venture but, when they got started, nobody was actually ready to put their money in.

Of course your friends and family want you to succeed. But if they are not your ideal target, is their positive excitement about your new solution relevant?

I was talking with my marketing manager, Vera, and she made a fantastic point about who you should listen to when it comes to market research. She said, 'I am interested in market research, but only from people that are willing to take their credit card out. Everything else is noise.' So instead of asking for feedback from everyone, focus on people who took their credit card out and voted for (by purchasing) your solution. Your company portfolio of clients is really the best way to understand your ideal clients. Rather than guessing who might be willing to pay for your solution, look at those who have already.

I recently had a client who claimed that 90% of his targeted clients were government authorities. When I asked to look at his last ten clients, the numbers were 60% government and 40% businesses. He realised that he should put more effort into the business sector and created additional marketing content to address it.

I went through this process with BizzBee Solutions and it helped me understand who we want to serve, and who our ideal client should be. As a management consulting company, we were quite generalist. Think of an industry and we've worked in it: HR, medical, healthcare, agriculture, IoT (internet of things), deep learning, elevator spare parts, hydrophilic polymers and many other niche industries that you've probably never heard of.

With each new client we had a lot to learn. We could only start to add value when we understood their industry, then their business. And we had 200 clients (at that time), which was many steep learning curves. We knew that defining our ideal client would mean that we could start adding value earlier.

From in-house analysis, we saw that we achieved fantastic results in the B2B segment, particularly for high-ticket service providers. We did OK in the other segments, and honestly failed to deliver in a few segments, but for B2B high-ticket service providers, we were working magic.

It is easy to see these patterns if you have ten clients in total; not so easy if you have hundreds. My first thought was to outsource or delegate the evaluation. But that won't work. You know your clients best, and you know things about them that are unique. I reluctantly got stuck into studying all 200 clients. It took me a few days, but the insights gave me confidence and strength to pursue my ICP.

If you have followed the guidelines in this section, you will now be at the starting point for defining your ICP: knowing the nature of your business, seeing the benefits of your solution and understanding your previous clients. Then you can look at the external world.

External forces

The second half of the task of identifying your ICP is to look outside, into the world, and understand who you should target.

It is easier to focus on internal analysis. If you already have several clients, you obviously did something right. But do you know if they are all ideal clients for you, or just random prospects that you serve? And how do you know that there aren't more ideal clients waiting for you out there?

For this second part of the equation, your key concern is how the market responds to your offer and why. When you look for external validation and try to understand who to target, there are always multiple variables. Otherwise, everyone would know who to target.

Instead of extensive external research, which could take months, use your findings on your strengths from the previous section to narrow and focus your research. Look at three main things: the market, the competition and the industry.

What are the market needs?

Can you find new market segments?

You've just identified the clients you have most enjoyed working with. Which are the top five to ten business profiles that you would love to work with? Regardless of what the stats and the market opportunity research say, you must love your target. There's no point in me telling you how to chase more profitable clients if you won't enjoy working with them. And since this decision (the opportunities you should pursue) will impact your entire company, you'd better focus on it now.

You also need to be an active listener and observer. There are opportunities all around us. Have you noticed a problem a company has? That's a business opportunity. Has someone told you about something they were struggling with? Another business opportunity.

But looking for opportunities anywhere and everywhere could drive you crazy, because there are so many out there. This is where you need to know your strengths, so that you can focus on the areas where you can offer the most help. And the more businesses you find with the same problem that you can solve, the better.

A client from Canada who offered a mix of training, masterclasses and courses on financial investment in options and futures came to me. He was targeting entrepreneurs and early business owners who wanted an extra income. That all sounded great, but when we did an ICP analysis we found some completely new markets, such as retired people who have plenty of free time and want to make some extra money. The client reshaped his marketing and grew his business exponentially.

Which other markets could benefit a lot from your offering? You may be surprised at what helpful answers this simple question can provide.

When I was looking at the BizzBee potential market, I focused on the services we offer. By talking to thousands of prospects, I realised there were a lot of market opportunities. Honestly, too many opportunities, making it harder for me to choose. But that is a nice headache to have, compared with the other extreme.

I was also working with a nongovernmental, not-for-profit association focused on supporting start-ups to help them understand the market needs. Although they had a reasonably well-defined ICP, they had missed some additional segments that they could address. We completed some market research and realised that there were a lot of business experts who had not yet considered starting their own businesses: a good market segment, with very specific needs. This was a great opportunity because nobody was targeting this segment, and although it is a long game, there are a lot of start-ups that are established by experienced specialists.

If you would like to know more about looking for market opportunities, I recommend *Business Model Generation* by Alexander Osterwalder[3] plus the frameworks PESTEL analysis,[4] Porter's Five Forces Analysis[5] and Blue Ocean,[6] which all focus on evaluating opportunities.

Is the target in the right industry?

Even when you identify a promising target, consider the future of that industry. If it is in a shrinking industry you should avoid it, even if it seems to be a promising marketing opportunity.

Plan for a long-term game rather than a quick win, and make sure you have the right industry in mind. It

---

3   A Osterwalder, *Business Model Generation* (John Wiley and Sons, 2010)
4   FJ Aguilar, *Scanning the Business Environment* (Macmillan, 1967)
5   ME Porter, 'How Competitive Forces Shape Strategy', *Harvard Business Review*, May 1979 (Vol. 57, No. 2), pp. 137–145, https://hbr.org/1979/03/how-competitive-forces-shape-strategy
6   W Chan Kim, *Blue Ocean Strategy* (Harvard Business Review Press, 2015)

is a pity to spend a lot of marketing effort on a dying industry, for example.

Let's take physical video rental. We all know the story of how Netflix replaced Blockbuster, but not everyone understands what happened after that. Netflix, as we know, created its own new industry: video streaming. Soon enough, competitors started catching up – Prime Video (Amazon), Hulu, Disney+ (The Walt Disney Company), YouTube (Google), HBO on Demand, Apple TV+ (Apple), Twitch (Amazon) and many more brands.

With all these big names, the industry matured quickly and became hard to compete in. Have you heard about Quibi?

Driven by the video-on-demand industry, Quibi was launched in April 2020 to target a younger demographic, with content delivered in ten-minute episodes. The service raised $1.75 billion from investors, and it was set for a great start. After six months, Quibi was shut down.[7] Of course the Covid-19 pandemic affected its projected revenues, but there was also the fact that it had entered a competitive industry, competing against a lot of big names.

Now back to you – what kind of market opportunities are available for your business? Which of those

---

7   B Heater, 'The Short, Strange Life of Quibi', TechCrunch, 2020,
     https://techcrunch.com/2020/10/23/the-short-strange-life-of-quibi

can you actually pursue, and put into action? Are the opportunities in a shrinking or growing industry? The answers to these questions will help you to choose better the right target for your business.

The next question: is the competition fierce, or nonexistent?

ANALYSING YOUR COMPETITION

Who are you up against?

Take a look at the businesses that are similar to yours – who are they targeting? Competition is healthy, but it could drive you out of business. There will always be competitors. What is important is how you respond to competition. Never underestimate the power of the insights you can get by looking at your competitors.

One approach is to see who your competitors are mainly targeting, and focus on the same client profile. If there are a lot of competitors around a certain market segment, it means that it is attractive, and you don't need to educate your target on the benefits. They are already problem-aware (they know that they have a problem) and solution-aware (they use some of the competitors' solutions). The concern here is that if there is a lot of competition, you would need to work hard to build your market share and prove how you are different or better. The key question would be how to differentiate yourself from your competitors in solving the target's problem.

Another approach uses the opposite logic: you study the kinds of clients your competitors target, and find a client profile that they are *not* targeting. This seems perfect at first sight, because you've found a market segment that is competitor-free. Ideal, right? But ask yourself *why* none of your competitors are targeting that market segment. Perhaps it is not big enough, is hard to work with or doesn't pay well. This is a risky move, but it could also be highly rewarding.

I worked with a client in cybersecurity. Like most companies in this area, we started targeting FinTech and online gambling as the industries in most need of cybersecurity. However, we realised that most cybersecurity companies were targeting the same industries. Even worse, many of the FinTech companies' founders were tech-intensive, with security as their core business, so were not willing to outsource.

After ICP research, we realised that retail and hospitals were the two most attractive options for cybersecurity services. They are not tech-intensive, and because tech is not their core business they are willing to delegate to a partner. They keep critical data and have an online presence. And they would be more willing to partner with a cybersecurity agency so that they can focus on their core business.

A third option to look at is benchmarking. This means looking at similar businesses to yours (even competitors) who are not serving the same market. If you are a consultant in the EU, for example, you can look at consultants in the US. You don't compete in the same market, but you can get some significant insight on who US consultants target and apply the same logic in the EU.

We had worked with a client from the US on creating in-depth market research for the modular housing industry. A few years later, we received a prospect from Romania in the same industry: modular housing. I took the same research approach and framework, because I already had a happy client in that sector. Instead of reinventing the wheel, I helped this client by using the insights gained with the previous project. As a result, the client from Romania realised that they could add additional services they were not aware of, and serve the exact same market segment. There was no conflict of interest because the businesses were serving different continents.

Looking at the market needs, the industry and the competition are healthy pointers to help you fine-tune your ideal target.

Fine-tune your ICP with LinkedIn

The kind of internal and external research and analysis introduced above takes a long time and there is a lot to digest. But if you want to grow your business, this level of effort and this stage of the ZZ Framework are essential.

Once you have identified your strengths and the available market opportunities, you are ready to create a list of several industries that best fit your business, and potential targets in those areas. Next you need to make some tough decisions to choose the clients that are most rewarding for you to serve: the flower patch with the sweetest nectar.

Don't be too rigid in defining your ICP. It's an iterative process. You set up a hypothesis, you test the hypothesis and if it is correct, you've got your ICP. If not, you adjust your hypothesis and try again. It is better to do this than spend months on analysis without making a decision.

Based on your strengths and the market opportunities, you might have between three and five ICPs that you can build your marketing and sales activities around (a different strategy for each one). I find LinkedIn Sales Navigator a useful tool to get an estimation of the initial size of the target audience and a great starting point to a more insightful ICP. LinkedIn's database of potential prospects never gets outdated or obsolete. People change jobs – they update their LinkedIn profile. People start a new business – they update their LinkedIn profile. By using LinkedIn, you tap into an up-to-date database of 760 million prospects and 30 million companies.

There are three elements to consider when searching for an ideal B2B client: the industry, the firmographics and the positions (the most relevant people for you to approach).

The right industry

You need to know by now which industry you want to work in. This will be hardest if you are a generalist, because the other types of business already have predefined industries.

Just knowing the industry is not enough, however. You need to target companies within the industry and keep fine-tuning the targeting process. The level of detail you go into depends on the nature of your business, but beware of ending up with a super-niche target profile that would not give you enough volume of business. This is why there is no single rule for defining your ICP.

For starters, look at the LinkedIn list of predefined industries that you can filter by. If we could define the whole ICP through existing LinkedIn filters, it would be much easier to build a database. But LinkedIn industry filters have limitations, so if you need a specific industry you might also need to use a keyword search.

For example, I created a campaign for BizzBee Solutions targeting SaaS (software-as-a-service). LinkedIn had filters for computer software, information services and information technology and services but I could not search for SaaS (because it is a type of business rather than an industry) so I had to refine the LinkedIn filters.

> **EXTRA HONEY: LINKEDIN INDUSTRY FILTERS**
> Find an updated list of LinkedIn industries on our resource page – www.BizzBeeSolutions.com/book-resources.

The right company

Once you have targeted your industry, you need to go deeper and define the firmographics: attributes of companies you might want to target, which can be used to gather individual firms into a meaningful market segment.

LinkedIn Sales Navigator has advanced filters that you can use to narrow the type of companies you want to target. Even better, it tells you instantly how many companies match your search criteria. If you get too many companies, you can tighten the search results by adding additional criteria. If too few, you can loosen up the search criteria.

A good starting point is the two most common criteria: geography (company location) and size (number of employees). When it comes to location, if you have a digital solution – don't worry. However, some companies have geographical constraints, so look at the geographical aspects of the potential clients. On LinkedIn, you can filter by cities, countries, regions, even continents. Play with the location filter to arrive at the right amount of companies to target.

Company size is important when defining your ICP. Working with start-ups and SMEs requires one type of effort, whereas working with corporations requires a completely different type. Differently sized companies face different types of problems, even in the same department. HR in a small business with ten to twenty employees is a completely different operation from an HR department in a business with 10,000 employees.

Based on the LinkedIn filters, you can reduce your target audience to a finite number – a number you can see and measure – and knowing the number of potential prospects will define your approach. It changes when you know whether your target is 500 companies or 50,000 companies.

If geography and company size are not specific enough, you can add additional criteria specific to your business. LinkedIn has filters related to department size, annual revenue, growth, followers, technologies used and so on. To make the firmographic aspect clear, I've made three examples of target searches using LinkedIn filters to show you how the number of target companies can vary depending on your ICP.

LINKEDIN TARGET SEARCH EXAMPLES

Client target 1	Client target 2	Client target 3
GEOGRAPHY: UNITED KINGDOM	GEOGRAPHY: UNITED STATES	GEOGRAPHY: AUSTRALIA
COMPANY HEADCOUNT: 1-10	COMPANY HEADCOUNT: 500+	COMPANY HEADCOUNT: <500
INDUSTRY: ACCOUNTING	INDUSTRY: MANAGEMENT CONSULTING	INDUSTRY: INFORMATION TECHNOLOGY
TARGET: 5,691 COMPANIES	TARGET: 341 COMPANIES	TARGET: 16,216 COMPANIES

The right people

Now that you have a clear idea of the companies you need to target, it's time to look at the last part of the puzzle – finding out who you are actually going to talk to. You need to find the positions that are the most relevant for you, their official titles, variations in positions and so on.

One of the key challenges in B2B sales is finding out who makes the buying decisions – what to buy, when and from whom. In contrast to B2C buying, the decisions usually involve more than just one or two people.

You can approach more than one person from the same department or even multiple people from different departments. But they all have different perspectives and concerns that you need to address, so they will each need a different approach and a different message from your sales and marketing process. It is common in a B2B outreach campaign to target multiple people and positions in the same company on the same subject, but approach them with different marketing messages.

For example, let's say you are offering an HR software solution. Although the most obvious approach would be to target HR positions, you can expand your approach as follows.

1. **HR decision-makers:** They know their stuff. They are problem-aware, solution-aware and probably already use software from your competition. You need to focus on the features and functionalities of your software compared with others on the market. You need to convince the software users that your software is superior, and it is worth the switch.

2. **Management decision-makers:** This could be the CEO, managing director, general manager or chief operating officer (COO). Here the approach should focus on how your software solution would help them make better company decisions, as well as how much easier their life would be thanks to all the software's reporting functionalities. See? They need HR software, but for different purposes.

3. **Financial decision-makers:** Not so obvious at first, but you can approach the chief financial officer (CFO), head of finance or financial director. They would be interested in how your HR software could save them a lot of money.

4. **IT decision-makers:** These are the people doing the magic behind the scenes. You need to help them understand how easy it is to integrate your software into their existing environment, and how effortless the entire process is. If you manage to do this, then you have a strong ambassador on your side.

So, as you can see, you can have different approaches for the same HR software.

When you are working out who to target, keep in mind that different industries have different position titles. There is no official title for each job role, and often people have multiple roles in the same company, making it difficult to distinguish exactly who you should target. That is why it is important to target variations of the role, so you can make sure that you are not missing someone.

How do you find out which positions are relevant for you? Again, you have to start with research and analysis. Look at product reviews, blogs or forums. Work out what kinds of people are commenting and posting, and what they are saying. Look at job descriptions, especially what responsibilities the job entails. You will often find out that you were targeting the wrong job positions. This is a lot of work, but it's all useful because you will familiarise yourself with your target industry and companies and better understand who you need to reach.

LinkedIn Sales Navigator includes advanced filters for seniority, job function and job title. You do not need to use all these all the time, but be aware of their existence. There are many additional filters you can use, but these three are the most common when looking for the right people to engage.

Function: If there's more than one department relevant to your solution, you will need to define an approach for each of them. LinkedIn gives you the option to search people by function, so you can select departments that you want to target. There are twenty-six job function filters available – sales, purchasing, marketing, legal, IT, HR and many more. You can find updated lists on our online resource page at www.BizzBeeSolutions.com/book-resources.

EXTRA HONEY:
LINKEDIN JOB FUNCTION FILTERS
There's a list of job function filters at www. BizzBeeSolutions.com/book-resources.

I usually use the function criteria when I am not sure of the exact job title I want to target, but I know the department. This can be useful in combination with the 'seniority level' filter.

Seniority level: Do you need to approach the owner of the company, the CEO or a director? Depending on your solution, you could decide to target several seniority levels. From lowest to highest, these are the levels LinkedIn allows you to set a filter for: Unpaid < Entry < Senior < Manager < Director < VP < CXO < Partner < Owner

So, for example, I can target function 'finance' and seniority 'director and above' to locate all the senior decision-makers in the finance department.

Title: The next step is to target your ideal position, with the specific job title, so you can better address specific role-related problems and benefits in your campaigns.

LinkedIn has a hidden secret in the job title search function: you can use Boolean search to include or exclude certain results. This allows you to use logical conjunctions AND, OR and NOT in your search.

You can also apply other search criteria – such as years in current position, years at current company, years of experience – to arrive at an even more specific ICP.

Do consider at this point whether the people you are trying to target are active enough online to receive your outreach: teachers, wellness practitioners, a lot of people in hospitality and hands-on clinical health professionals spend most of their time working offline. You might have to consider reaching them through another level of their organisation.

Not all ICP criteria can fit the existing LinkedIn filters, of course, and in many cases you will need to look for leads outside LinkedIn. However, LinkedIn is a great tool to give you an indication of the initial size of the target audience and a starting point to a more insightful ICP.

Conversation starters: how to engage your target

If you have followed the ZZ Framework to this point, you have defined your ICP, or even several of them. You probably feel ready to plan your marketing outreach, and are excited to start working on the touchpoints, messaging, etc. Wait a little longer – there is one more step first.

To get your ICP to respond to your campaign, you need to create messages that resonate with them. Conversion depends on creating a message that provokes emotions (fear, happiness) or presents an opportunity. Sending a generic message invalidates all the work you have done to this point. Why bother defining your ICP if you then spam them with generic content?

The main purpose of the ICP is to define who you want to approach and create ultra-specific content for that target, whether it is inbound (e-book, landing page, article, SEO) or outbound (LinkedIn messaging, email, cold calling). You need to complete another layer of research – but this time it's specific and narrow. Understanding three layers of problems and opportunities relevant to your target will help you create better conversation starters. These are:

1. Related to their position

2. Related to the type of company they are in

3. About the industry they are in

Position-specific problems are directly relevant to your target person. What kind of day-to-day problems do they face at work? Are their struggles team-related? Is it hard for them to get financial approval? Do they have to prepare frequent and lengthy reports?

Identify the top three to five problems or struggles your target position experiences, and document them. You will need this information later, when you create conversation starters.

As a founder of a bootstrapped consulting company, I can divulge that my main fear was not ensuring enough revenue to cover our monthly costs and not having some extra for investment in growth. If someone approached me with, 'I know it is hard to run a business without knowing whether you will exist in three months,' they would capture my attention because they obviously understood my pain. But if the same message was sent to a founder who received a lot of funding, then it would not resonate. It is key to find the right topics to discuss based on who you target.

To do this, you need to research, read blogs, visit forums and find out what people are complaining about. This is the only way to learn more about your

ICP. Yes, it will help with your messaging, and on a deeper level it will aid a better understanding of the clients you serve.

Company-specific problems are not specific to a single company, but specific to the criteria you've selected as relevant for firmographics – company size, location, industry, etc. What particular problems do these kinds of companies have? These issues won't get the same attention as position-specific ones about your target's daily troubles, but they still show that you know and understand the company.

For example, BizzBee Solutions, a company with up to fifty employees working in the management consulting industry, is based in Macedonia. Macedonia does not support PayPal and Stripe, meaning that we can only use bank transfers and credit card payments when we work with international clients. We share this problem with all other companies of a similar size in Macedonia (or other countries not supported by PayPal or Stripe).

Take a look at the companies you've shortlisted as an ideal target. What kind of problems do they have? Can you search and identify a few key concerns?

Industry-specific problems need to be in your outreach arsenal, although they might not immediately affect the targeted companies or individuals. These should be your last resort.

Considering my business again, BizzBee Solutions has a problem that is typical in the management consulting industry: companies are not always keen to pay for advice, research, access to knowledge or other intangible offerings. You have to experience our service to know whether it is of benefit to you. We try to overcome that problem by providing social proof – we have a 'wall of love' section on our website (www. BizzBeeSolutions.com/bee-wall-of-love) with more than 400 client testimonials and plenty of case studies. But this remains a problem for our industry in general.

With all this in mind, you should be able to do focused research to identify position-specific problems, company-level problems and industry-level problems relevant to your ICP. These will help you to grab attention by introducing the right topics in your messages.

Having a defined ICP will make every aspect of your outreach more efficient – from building a database of targeted prospects and creating tailored messages, to executing successful LinkedIn and email campaigns.

At the end of this chapter you will find an updated framework, including the subframeworks.

Chapter takeaway

Now you know why I said that doing a B2B ICP is not a walk in the park, but all the guidance you need is in this chapter. Here's a quick recap.

Start with the **internal forces**. Define the type of business you are, what kind of benefits you deliver and what insight you can draw from your existing and former clients.

Then move to the **external forces**. Looking at existing market needs, the maturity of the industry and the competition should give you a good idea of who to target.

Based on these two pieces of research, you can start defining your **ICP**. Start with the target industry, then look at different firmographics (like company location, size, etc), and based on the job title, seniority and job function define the target positions within the company (the people you want to reach).

Finally, look into potential **conversation starters**, starting from position-specific and company-specific issues and finishing with industry-specific topics.

The image below looks quite complex, but it is just a representation of the steps you have followed in this chapter.

FLOWER SCOUTING FRAMEWORK
FOR ICP-DEFINING

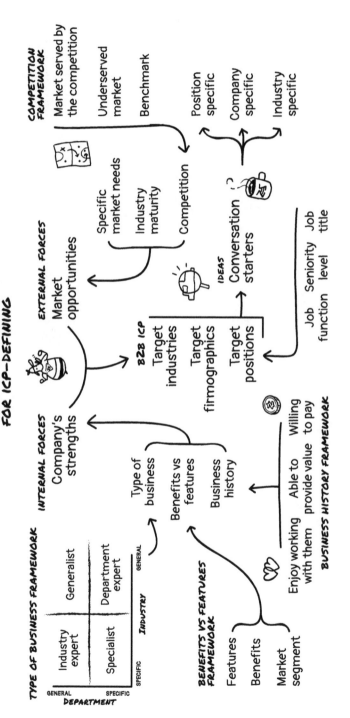

TYPE OF BUSINESS FRAMEWORK

	GENERAL	SPECIFIC
SPECIFIC	Industry expert	Specialist
GENERAL	Generalist	Department expert

GENERAL ⟷ SPECIFIC
DEPARTMENT

SPECIFIC / INDUSTRY / GENERAL

INTERNAL FORCES
Company's strengths
- Type of business
- Benefits vs features
- Business history

EXTERNAL FORCES
Market opportunities
- Specific market needs
- Industry maturity
- Competition

COMPETITION FRAMEWORK
- Market served by the competition
- Underserved market
- Benchmark
- Position specific
- Company specific
- Industry specific

B2B ICP
- Target industries
- Target firmographics
- Target positions

IDEAS
Conversation starters
- Job function
- Seniority level
- Job title

BUSINESS HISTORY FRAMEWORK
- Enjoy working with them
- Able to provide value
- Willing to pay

BENEFITS VS FEATURES FRAMEWORK
- Features
- Benefits
- Market segment

2
Database
(Nectar Collection)

The database framework

Bees collect nectar for two reasons – for their immediate
needs (to feed themselves) and to store for the future (to
make honey). It provides immediate energy for the bee
in the form of carbohydrate sugars and the bee stores the
excess nectar in its stomach to take it back to the hive.

Once back at the hive, the nectar is passed between the
worker bees. You don't want to know how this happens. Excess water evaporates as it's passed around the
bees and finally an enzyme in a bee's stomach turns the
more concentrated sugar into raw honey. Then honey
production begins – a whole new task and a whole different chapter. The critical point in this chapter is making sure that the nectar has reached the honey stomach.

Making a prospects database is also a long process (but slightly less revolting) in which the nectar (the prospects that you have gathered from your most promising flower patch, full of pollen-rich blooms that fit your ICP) is handed from the database-building bees to the execution bees.

The quality of the outreach in the next step will inevitably depend on both the type of flowers where the pollen was harvested and the sweetness of the nectar – the quality of the defined ICP and the database. So how do you make sure that your nectar (data) is good enough to turn into honey?

Database-building can be a pain in the neck. But, whether you are an owner or part of a sales team, you will have to source leads for your product or solution. For an automated LinkedIn-only campaign, it is possible that you may not need to create a database. This would save a lot of time, but there are a few downsides, which I will discuss soon.

Yes, you should use a range of other channels – building landing pages and offering digital assets, creating content for boosting SEO, paying for ads to bring traffic. But while waiting for those efforts to yield results, you also need to proactively look for potential clients.

From a marketing perspective, the primary purpose of a database of highly targeted leads is, indeed, for an outreach campaign. But there is so much more that can be done with the list. You can create tailored blogs, a white paper or an e-book and share them with the list. You can build a newsletter for your prospects based around specific topics of value to them.

From a sales perspective, you can use your list to build relationships with target companies and people. This is not a quick win: it is a highly crafted approach to bring the prospect closer to you and your business. Knowing their pain points, and having researched your conversation starters, you can reach out to them with a customised approach. A database helps you focus on relationship-building and closing, rather than prospecting.

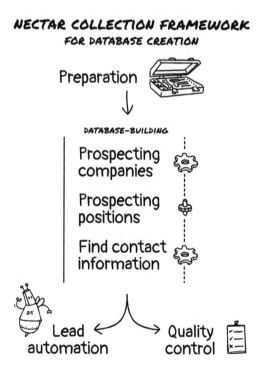

NECTAR COLLECTION FRAMEWORK
FOR DATABASE CREATION

Preparation

DATABASE-BUILDING

Prospecting companies

Prospecting positions

Find contact information

Lead automation ← → Quality control

1. **Preparation:** Before you start, ensure you have a clear understanding of who you want in your database and who you don't (your ICP). There are a few tools and spreadsheets that can help you.

2. **Prospect companies:** This covers everything you need to know to find your ideal client companies. It involves mostly using search engines, but also many other techniques and approaches.

3. **Find the right people:** Don't contact the CEO for everything and wonder why you never get a response. For example, if you have an HR solution, consider adding the HR decision-makers or maybe even the financial and IT decision-makers to the targeting mix (as discussed in the previous chapter). Find the positions within the company that are concerned with what you have to offer.

4. **Find contact information:** Don't be the person who always emails companies using their generic email. Learn how to find direct contact information – direct business emails, direct phone numbers and LinkedIn profiles.

5. **Lead automation:** Once you know how to do the prospecting yourself, then you can consider automation tools. There is not a single solution that can solve your prospecting problem – often what's needed is a mix of tools that can partially automate your process, but rarely 100% of it. We are continuously screening the web for new

automation tools; we test their accuracy and rarely find any are more than 70–80% accurate.

6. **Quality control:** Database-building is always prone to mistakes, whether human (typos) or computer mistakes (tools are not always 100% accurate). You must go through several steps to ensure that you have the highest quality list.

Based on our experience, and inspired by the bee analogy, we have developed our nectar collection framework for database creation that will help you build a perfect list of prospects.

Preparation: before you start prospecting

Honestly, database-building is the most labour-intensive step of all. That's why it is left to the worker bees. And it is so important, because if you don't have an exceptional database of potential prospects you will not get results from your outreach, whatever you write or do.

To help you, here are a few preparatory steps to set up your environment for lead generation and make your database-building as efficient as possible.

At this stage in the ZZ Framework you understand your ICP thanks to the research from the previous chapter, and have identified your ideal target. Now you need to be clear about what kind of information you want to collect on each prospect.

It helps to set up an efficient environment. And you can start by installing some tools and extensions to save you time.

Extensive ICP understanding

Most of the 400-plus clients I have talked to either did not know their ICP when they came to us, or needed further clarification. I have spent a lot of time and effort convincing clients that building a database is meaningless without having a clear ICP.

For example, I was coaching an HR agency eager to start using outreach to get new clients from the EU. They had more than ten years' experience and a raft of services, helping companies with restructuring, employee evaluation and teambuilding, with a final outcome of increasing productivity, reducing costs and retaining employees.

My first question was, 'Knowing your ICP, are we building a database of target clients or partners?'

And that was a dilemma. Targeting clients means a lot of effort in outreach and sales, but the profit margin is quite high. If you target partners, you are pursuing collaboration, offering win-win to potential partners, giving you significantly better results from your outreach. Your partners might take care of client relationships, marketing and sales, and can bring you more than one client. On the other hand, working with partners means a much smaller profit margin. A real dilemma, which my client the HR agency needed time to think about.

My second question for the agency was, 'Knowing your ICP, are we building a database of high-priced product/services, or high-turnover product/services?'

And that was another dilemma. Targeting high-ticket (expensive) service providers (software development companies, consultants, etc) means that the sales cycle will be slower, and it would require a more complex sales process and premium price. On the other hand, if you target high-turnover product/services (eg food manufacturing), you need a completely different sales approach. But most importantly, the HR agency's service (restructuring, employee evaluation, teambuilding, etc) would be completely different based on these two directions.

My final question was, 'Which of the services you offer would be the easiest way into the target company?' You can't really base your outreach on more than twenty services. You need a laser-focused approach, with the service that is most attractive. Once you start collaborating with a client, if they see the value, you have unlimited possibilities for offering additional services. But at the beginning, offering too many services will potentially confuse the prospect and weaken your message sequence.

This is just one example of how you might struggle to choose which service or solution to focus on, and exactly what you want to achieve. It is a common problem for agencies and development companies.

EXTRA HONEY: WHAT DATA DO YOU NEED?

We created a one-page questionnaire to help us understand our new clients' targets, as well as the type of data needed for company, position and contact information.

If you cannot answer the questions, have another look at the previous chapter on the ICP before you approach database-building.

Find the questionnaire at www.BizzBeeSolutions.com/book-resources.

Let's imagine you are a new client of BizzBee and you want us to help you with lead generation. This is what you would need to know before we can really start helping you.

1. **Basic info about your company and target service:** I know you already know this. But we've found it is useful to let the client tell us as much as possible about themselves, especially about the

target service that will be used for the outreach. Think about what your business is about and who you are trying to serve and how, as if you were doing a presentation (we actually ask new clients to do presentations for us).

2. **Target company info:** Finding the right companies to target is crucial, so you need to know all the specifics we discussed in the previous chapter: industries, locations and employee range. Now you are looking in detail at the pieces of information needed per company, in terms of columns needed for each prospect. It can be company name, website, address, generic email address and other specific fields that will help your business.

   Also you need to define how many target companies you are planning on reaching out to. It is easy to say 'all', but if there are 20,000, you might need to consider batches to reach them all – at the beginning.

3. **Target position info:** Here you need to state who you want to reach out to. It can be a management decision-maker (CEO, managing director, chief operations officer), financial decision-maker, HR decision-maker or IT, etc.

   In many cases you should define alternative positions, remembering that different industries name the same roles differently. I also recommend going after several people in each company.

Reaching out to five people from the same company can have far greater impact than reaching out to just one.

The last step is to decide what kind of information you want to collect on each prospect. Once all this is clear, you can focus your database-building effort.

Each piece of information should be a separate column. Too many columns mean a lot of effort in database-building. But too little data could significantly affect your results. Choose wisely.

Prepare your environment

After you have decided what information you need in the database, prepare the spreadsheet in which you will collect and store the prospects. I recommend a Google spreadsheet, because you can access it from anywhere – computer, phone, guest computer – plus you can share it with a team, and it allows multiple entries in parallel. More than five people can work at the same time on the same spreadsheet, without worrying about overlapping, versioning, etc. For example, we used a Google spreadsheet to build a database of 11,000 prospects of ecommerce decision-makers for an SEO agency. As the timeline was short, we needed a lot of people to work in parallel.

Do take account of human error when using spreadsheets, which is more likely if multiple people are working at the same time. It's easy to mistype something, enter data in the wrong place or miss something important. We therefore built an in-house lead generation template spreadsheet that prevents typos or duplication in the prospect list.

EXTRA HONEY:
LEAD GENERATION SPREADSHEET
The BizzBee bulletproof lead generation spreadsheet template is on our resources page – www. BizzBeeSolutions.com/book-resources

So we now have a bulletproof template that solves 99% of the problems that were reported by our clients. Our spreadsheet is all set up with categories and formulas. Set up yours according to the information that will be most useful to you. For example, if you need a website, name of the company, location, but not the number of employees and industry and the other categories, delete those. There are also spare columns in case you need to add others. In the board tab, there are counters and 'spreadsheet signalisation' to help you navigate through the info and data you enter.

If you are using customer relationship management software, like Salesforce, Microsoft Dynamics or HubSpot, you can work directly in the CRM. It will enable you to add the data in fields, and if you enter the website or the domain, it can pre-fill a lot of additional data for the person or company. However, we've tried the CRM route several times with clients and found that it was easier to build a database than work with the CRM and its predefined steps. Each CRM has own environment, with extra fields, and can be hard to navigate. A spreadsheet is a simple table that you can enrich, qualify and update. From experience, it is better to work in a spreadsheet to build the initial database of prospects. When you do your last step, the quality check, however, I encourage you to upload the database to the CRM, because the CRM will help you track your progress with each lead.

When setting up the environment, you also need some **tools** that can help you during the prospecting process.

If you don't already have a Google account, create one so that you can align your Gmail profile with a Google Chrome profile. Some of the tools that we use are Chrome extensions, which will save you a lot of time.

A LinkedIn account is also essential.

EXTRA HONEY: HANDY CHROME EXTENSIONS
Chrome extensions change a lot so we will put a frequently updated list on our resource page: www.BizzBeeSolutions.com/book-resources.

Prospecting: find the right companies

Let's dive in and help you find a list of companies that match your criteria.

Prospecting companies requires three steps:

1. Obtaining lists of companies from various sources

2. Qualifying whether they are relevant for you

3. Collecting the information you need in your database

LinkedIn Sales Navigator is the leading tool for finding companies, with its searchable database of 30 million companies. (You can get a free one-month trial to see what it can do for you.) Based on your ICP, filter out companies by country / region, industry and number of employees.

For an automated LinkedIn-only campaign, you could just use the Sales Navigator filters to point out your ICP and set up your automation tool to start reaching out to them.

This would save a lot of time, but there are downsides. When you build a database you qualify each prospect, and confirm that they are relevant. When using LinkedIn filters only, there could be prospects that are there by mistake.

Plus, as I said before, LinkedIn has limitations. It has predefined industry filters, and some industries are not included. Let me show you a few examples.

- A client from Australia, targeting yoga and personal training centres in Melbourne, Australia

- A marketing agency in the UK, prospecting private dentists

- A shopping optimisation technology platform from Germany, targeting ecommerce companies; a digital innovation agency from Australia had the same target

Unfortunately, LinkedIn does not have these industries as options. You can use the advanced search filters, but it also requires manual work to ensure that the companies shortlisted by LinkedIn are relevant for your campaign.

When LinkedIn cannot give you the desired results, look at the alternative B2B databases available.

Yellow Pages/Yelp is helpful in cases where you are more interested in local companies, or industries that aren't available on LinkedIn, and includes searching by industry, subindustry and location. We had success using Yellow Pages with a UK client offering branded all-in-one point-of-sale (POS) solutions for restaurants and were able to prospect restaurants within specific geographical areas. The limitation is that it's not possible to use additional search parameters like number of employees, so it is necessary to manually research the shortlisted companies to ensure they fit the rest of your criteria.

Here are some other options, but they are more complex or need manual validating.

Google Maps lets you search for a specific company type in a region and find physical locations of targeted companies. This is useful when the nature of your business is limited by city or region.

Associations or **NGOs** that work in the same field/ industry often keep publicly available lists of their members; for us that means industry-specific potential target companies.

Fairs and **exhibitions** in the relevant industry show a list of their participants, sometimes even with contact details.

Government databases: if you are targeting regulated industries (eg banks or insurance companies), they must have a licence to operate and the government has a database of licensed entities. In addition, some governments make company records public. For example, Companies House in the UK has publicly available information on all companies established in the UK.

Depending on your target, there are **platforms** that specialise in a specific segment. For example, Booking.com can give you comprehensive access to hotels and accommodation businesses. Is there a platform for your industry?

As a last resort, do a Google search for specific industries or regions.

There are also many **pre-existing databases** that you can use: ZoomInfo, Hoovers, Crunchbase and Angel.co are just a few. Each has a unique angle on the company search, whether geographically, departmentally or at what stage the companies are. Combined, they have hundreds of millions of companies available via different categorisations or search filters.

The goal of this step is to find enough companies that could potentially be your clients. This is a great starting point, but you don't know yet that all the companies you have shortlisted are relevant. You now move to the next step, choosing those most likely to become your clients.

EXTRA HONEY: DATABASE LIST

Check out our resource section for the latest database list: www.BizzBeeSolutions.com/book-resources.

For companies that have a broader target, there may be no need for further qualification – especially if you are targeting all restaurants in a particular area, or all companies within defined LinkedIn filters (eg accounting companies in the UK with ten to fifty employees). In this case, through these sources, you will be able to extract a list of companies that all have great potential to become a client.

However, some companies have a narrower target. And this is not only about firmographics. A social media marketing agency that came to us specialised in the sports industry. Their key qualification was that the target companies should only have a limited social media presence, which narrowed down the list significantly.

Another client was an investment company in renewable energy, particularly solar energy, interested in UK companies with large rooftops (a total roof space of 16,000 m^2 or more). Anything below that was not feasible for them.

We used Google Maps to search for larger real estate projects, usually around airports and industrial zones. We used some external tools to measure the area of an object on Google Maps. We were not left with a lot of potential companies – but all of them were highly relevant for the client. These show how putting effort into qualification can make a huge difference.

If you disqualify the nonrelevant companies at this stage, you won't waste time adding them to the database or looking for contact information. You can focus on the companies that are more likely to become your client.

Once a company matches your qualification criteria, add it to your spreadsheet. Then you **enrich the company** with the key information you need. The company fields can be basic info about the company: company name, website, generic email. However, as the example above showed, you might want to add more information, such as number of social posts on all social media in the last week/month, total years in existence or even rooftop size of the building.

Prospecting: Find the right people

Once the list of companies is qualified and enriched, the next step is to find the people you need to approach within these companies.

When looking for targeted positions, you follow the same targeting framework as with the companies – obtain lists of people from various sources, confirm whether they are relevant for you and collect the necessary information into the database. Get these three steps right to ensure you're reaching out to the right people.

LinkedIn Sales Navigator is still the best source. Nearly every large company has a LinkedIn profile. Once you know the company, you can research its employees, or you can look for the required position within the company. This is by far the most efficient way to find target positions within a specific company.

Sometimes the company is not on LinkedIn. Perhaps small, local companies do not have a LinkedIn profile. Or if they do, the employees don't have a LinkedIn account. Try looking at the company website. Usually there are pages like About Us, Contact Us or Meet the Team where you can find the staff with their email, phone number or social media links. The company blog section is also a good place to look, especially if you are looking for marketing decision-makers or CEOs. Blog posts are often written by the CEO or quote the CEO.

While working on projects targeting yoga, fitness and small ecommerce companies, we mostly use company websites and social media pages.

The next source is Google. You can search for 'company name' + 'target position' and look at the results from the first page. In many cases, Google will point out news, an event or anything where that specific position is mentioned, followed by the name and surname. Just be careful: you need recent, updated data, not the CEO who retired ten years ago.

The smaller the companies you are targeting, the less information will be online. It also varies by the industry. Regulated businesses (like banks or insurance companies) and IT-literate businesses (software, telecoms, agencies) will have much more information about their employees online than agriculture, manufacturing, wholesale or import/export companies. Public companies are the perfect target – because they have an investor section, where they have to disclose everything.

Once you have multiple potential people from the same company, the next step is to **qualify** them. If you target bigger companies, you will find several people in the same roles (eg marketing manager), and you will need to look deeper to understand who is the best fit for your ICP.

Just as with the company qualification, this depends on your business. If you have broader criteria, you can target all the people with the same or similar job position from the same company.

When we worked with a marketing and PR technology stack company from Finland, we were targeting all marketing decision-makers from a particular industry. Some companies had between five and ten marketing decision-makers: marketing managers, marketing director, chief marketing officer (CMO), head of marketing, VP of marketing. And there was no need for additional qualification for these positions.

However, if you have more narrow criteria, you will need to qualify each person individually.

There are cases where you can target multiple people from the same company, but within different departments.

For one of our clients, we were looking for four employees per company, but only one per department – to reach the various departments with different messaging. The client was looking at:

1. Top-level executives (CEO, managing director, etc)

2. Titles related to procurement (purchasing director, commercial director, head of purchasing, etc)

3. Financial executives (financial director, CFO, etc)

4. Facility-related roles (facilities manager, site manager, property manager, etc)

The key was to add all of them in 'cc' when emailing, to trigger a psychology effect and increase the response rate.

If you are only going to reach out to one person per department, you do need to qualify them and make sure you have the right person. Depending on your business, you might need to qualify people based on a geographical location, especially if you are targeting bigger companies and corporations with multiple locations. In this case, there are several people with the same role, each responsible for a different geographical area. In many cases looking at the title is not enough. You need to read the job description to understand whether the person is a good fit.

Remember, your purpose here is to disqualify the nonrelevant people, and focus on those who are right for you, with the end result of adding three to five people per company.

Finally, once the person matches your qualification criteria, you can add them into the spreadsheet. You can then **enrich** the person with the key information you need.

Based on your business, the data information can be more generic – name, surname, job title. You could add some additional fields particularly relevant for you – years within the company, where they worked previously, whether they were promoted to the current role or directly hired. This data will help you know them better, and improve your outreach.

Prospecting: Find their contact information

In most cases, the primary contact information is the person's business email. Next, we encourage you to find their LinkedIn profile so you can connect on a more informal/chatty channel. Having their direct phone number is quite useful as well – although, from experience, finding direct phone numbers is not as easy as finding emails and LinkedIn profiles. Depending on your solution, you might want their other social media platforms – Facebook, Twitter, Instagram, etc. And remember, you don't want a generic company email address, but a direct email for the most relevant person you can target.

There are several ways you can find personal contact information. There are many tools, scrapers and email finders, as well as databases, and more appearing every day. Our updated list of scrapers is available at www.BizzBeeSolutions.com/book-resources.

Here are a few other strategies and tricks to help you.

The first and most obvious one is to **check the company website**, especially the regular About Us/Contact Us/Meet the Team pages. I've also found the Imprint page useful, especially for German companies. It's where companies often state the names of the decision-making team and their contact information.

Another approach is to look for any email from that company and **work out the email pattern** that the company uses: Name.Surname@domain.com and so on. You can then apply that pattern to the person you need.

There are several **Chrome extensions** that can help you screen the company website and see all the existing emails on the web. Hunter.io, Findthatlead.com and many more are listed on our resources sheet at www.BizzBeeSolutions.com/book-resources.

A simple **Google search** can also do the trick. Searching for 'Dancho Dimkov' + 'email', I was able to find my email in the first page of search results. There is a high chance that the target person has left their email somewhere, as a participant in an event or conference, as part of a promotional leaflet or ad, or even on a forum/blog.

When looking for a business email, keep in mind that international companies have several domains, like .com, .com.mk, .co.uk, .fr, .net, .org, .nl.com, .sk.com, or they might have a different domain for each country that they operate in. And the emails for employees based in that country might be within that domain, rather than on the international domain.

A Google search might also yield social media profiles and direct phone numbers, if they are not on the company website.

It takes time and practice to master these strategies. Once you identify which sources and patterns work best for your target audience, you might choose to hire a dedicated team for database creation, outsource the workload to an external agency that specialises in database creation or use automation for the process.

How can you automate prospecting?

Now is a great time for me to address the automation issue. The entire database creation can be done without automation. Many corporations hire BDRs or data specialists whose core role is to create a database of highly targeted leads.

However, small service providers don't have the capacity or resources to do this on their own. As a software company, or an agency, your focus is to serve clients, and not dedicate your team to database-building. And automation, although it is not perfect, might be considered good value for money – saving precious time. Don't try it before you understand the basics of prospecting, because using scrapers and knowing which scraper to use for which purpose is an art on its own. You risk catching the digital outreach fever. You can get lost in all the options that scrapers offer, and may be unable to judge whether the scraper delivered on its promise. Also, if you don't understand the process, how will you know which scraper to use?

When you think about automation, instead of thinking about tools, think about your business processes. Not whether you can or can't use automation, but rather what can be automated at which step. For example, when looking for companies on LinkedIn, you can save a lot of time by using a tool to collect the company info into a spreadsheet. But you will need to finish the qualification stage manually.

If researching positions, you can use some degree of automation but if you have custom fields that you want for each person, you will have to do it manually. Think about automating certain processes rather than the whole project.

EXTRA HONEY: MY SCRAPERS GUIDE AND AUTOMATION CASE STUDIES

I compared more than a hundred scrapers from the web. Each had their advantages and disadvantages or focused on specific aspects instead of providing complete prospecting solutions.

You will find a frequently updated list of more than forty scrapers on our online resources page: www. BizzBeeSolutions.com/book-resources.

It would take too much space to evaluate them all, and it is practically impossible to compare them. Each tool has its own benefits and, depending on your needs, brings a different value. I've created three case studies to show how automation can save you significant time in finding the companies, finding the right people and finding their contact information. I walk you through the process on the resources page: www.BizzBeeSolutions.com/book-resources.

Quality control

All this effort can go to waste if you don't complete a quality check. It is not good if you get people's names wrong, or if the majority of your emails bounce (which could raise red flags with your email service provider).

Using the **spreadsheet template** provided earlier helps remove the most common human errors. For example, if you leave an empty space in a cell or forget to put @ in the email section, the spreadsheet will pick that up. If you add a Gmail or Yahoo email, or any other non-business email, it will also colour-code it to show you that it is a personal email rather than a business one.

The main goal of this spreadsheet is to reduce mistakes, but a spreadsheet is not able to tell you whether the email is correct or whether it will bounce. For that purpose, there are other tools that specialise in email verification. A simple Google search for 'email checker' or 'bulk email verify' will give you a lot of options. Also, many of the automation tools mentioned in this chapter have incorporated email verification. Let's dive into a bit more technical stuff.

Email verification checks for spam traps (email created to capture senders); it formats and does a syntax check (missing @ or double @@), verifies domains (DNS records) and validates individual mailboxes (SMTP protocol). Next, it filters all emails against a constantly updated list of 780+ disposable email providers and your accounts' blacklisted addresses to remove any previously failed addresses. The system will also check for invalid DNS entries and filter generic departmental accounts such as marketing@domain.com. Last, it performs a deep-cleaning SMTP test that will connect to the destination mail server and check whether that mailbox exists and is able to receive mail.

This all sounds a bit technical, but trust me – all you need to do is upload the database, and in return you will get a list of green (passed), yellow (unknown) and red (failed) emails.

Compliance with data privacy regulations is also important. In the EU, the GDPR (General Data Protection Regulation) has been compulsory since May 2018. In the US is the US Privacy Law, while Australia has the Australian Privacy Act 1988. When you do manual data creation, you are searching publicly available data on the company and the individual, looking at contact information on their website, LinkedIn, Google. When you use automation tools, to be / remain compliant you need to check that the tools are compliant, too.

Chapter takeaway

Building a database of highly qualified leads requires a lot of effort. But done properly, it is worth it.

You start with **defining the data** needed and setting up the prospecting environment. What information do you need for each company and position, and what contact information?

Next you build the database with **targeted companies**. Based on the available sources and lists, you qualify whether the companies are relevant to you. Then you enrich the entry with all the extra information needed.

Afterwards, you look for the **right people** within the companies. From different sources you locate relevant roles and positions. After qualification, you add them to your database and enrich with the extra information needed.

Only then can you start looking at the **contact information**. Finding direct email, phone and social media profiles will always help execute a better outreach.

Automation tools, scrapers and data improvement tools can help make your database-building faster and more efficient but you will need a mix of tools tailored to your business – there is no unified solution for all companies.

Finally, you need **quality control** over the database, to ensure maximum deliverability, as well as ensuring compliance with privacy laws and GDPR or whatever applies in your situation.

NECTAR COLLECTION FRAMEWORK
FOR DATABASE CREATION

Data needed

Environment set-up

Preparation

DATABASE-BUILDING

Prospecting companies

Prospecting positions

Find contact information

Sources of companies & positions

Qualification

Data enrichment

Lead automation

Quality control

Deliverability

GDPR

3
Copy
(Honeycomb Creation)

The copy framework

A suitable environment is a prerequisite for growth. Bees have maybe one of the most aesthetically pleasing home interiors in nature: the honeycomb.

Why do bees build themselves these exquisite homes? Well, the most apparent and well-known reason is that the honeycomb is the perfect place to create and store honey.

Its concise hexagonal pattern is a symbol for structure, order, utility and strength. This hasn't occurred by chance. Compared with the other shapes that leave no gaps (such as triangles and squares), the hexagon creates a comb with the least amount of structural material – ie wax.

This way, the bees produce the most value with the least effort. It can take between a week and two months for bees to build their honeycomb. But the end result is astonishing.

Just as each individual hexagonal cell has a story to tell through the various ways in which bees can use it, so each of your messages can resonate differently with each recipient. What should you do to make your copy as pleasing and as compelling as a honeycomb? You need a solid structure to produce that sweet honey that we know as brand new clients.

In 2021 I started a video podcast, talking to the creators of LinkedIn and email marketing automation tools about what inspired them to build these tools and how they can help us be more efficient in reaching out to a cold prospect on LinkedIn or email. The interviews are still available on BizzBee's website at www.BizzBeeSolutions.com/video-interviews.

The owners I spoke to shared one strong message – the quality of your copy is the single most important factor in outreach. You can have the best identified ICP and build the best possible database, but with a weak message or spammy content you won't get far. And this comes from the people who know: founders of marketing and sales tools who oversee thousands of outreach campaigns and have access to all client metrics.

When I first decided to try outreach, I was sceptical and embarrassed about having to use it, as a consultant. So I know some of my fellow consultants might find this uncomfortable as well. They might feel it diminishes their brand if they, as experts, reach out to potential clients. But the contact can be relationship-building and authority-building rather than salesy or pitchy.

The same applies to software owners. Reaching out does not undervalue your software. It is about building a database of companies that share a problem – one that you can solve.

Back then, clients were coming to me thanks to the other channels that I used, but it wasn't enough. I had to be proactive. In the beginning, I was sending out a single email or LinkedIn message: a longer one, showing all the services I had. And, obviously, it did not work.

When people did not respond, I tried harder – showing even more of my services, and how they could benefit from them. My outreach technique developed into several emails or messages outlining my best aspects of my services. My hopes went up.

Silence.

I only saw results when I started to figure out how to intrigue people and draw them into conversation. Crafting messages for outreach is an art – finding the combination of words that engages the prospect and makes them curious. B2B outreach copywriting is a small, ignored segment in the copywriting world, which I believe should get far more attention. If you are reaching out as a high-ticket service provider, it is even more specialist.

The first thing you need to learn about outreach copy is obvious when you think about it. People assume that if you create the perfect copy, clients will line up to buy your solution. But message creation for cold prospecting is not the same as message creation for sales.

When approaching a cold lead, your one and only goal is to get engagement and start a conversation. Nothing more. You are definitely not trying to pitch or make a sale, just get the prospect to engage in a conversation. Not about the weather (although that is also a good conversation starter), but in the area of your expertise.

If you are a cybersecurity consultant, you want to get your cold prospect talking about how safe they feel their digital world is. If you have a SaaS in contract management, you might start a conversation about how the procurement team handles and organises its contracts. If you handle the conversation in the right way, you will get responses. See Chapter 5 on Nurture (honey tasting) for what to do when your prospects respond.

Too many people try to sell directly to cold prospects: 'Hi, my name is Dancho, and I [value proposition]. Would you be interested in a call?'

I receive this kind of message too frequently. And it doesn't work. When you reach out to cold prospects, their guard is up and they're sceptical about what you have to say. This is why we get plenty of irrelevant emails in our inbox and also why we instantly delete them. Would you buy something from an unknown company that has just sent you an email? Especially an expensive service? Probably not.

People have become used to getting reams of spam messages trying to sell them anything and everything. Their guard is up when someone approaches them for anything. So the sales pitch approach to cold prospects no longer works – the approach needs to be more of a conversation. Try to get to know the person. Become a friend. Then qualify the contact (are they really your ideal client?) and invite them to a discovery/sales call *only* if it would be relevant.

This chapter focuses on the top layer of the funnel – creating a sequence of messages that will motivate your cold prospect to engage in a conversation. And again, that is your sole purpose; nothing more.

Depending on the time and resources available, you need to decide on the number of message sequences. If you can, craft different message sequences for each target job role (HR, management, finance). This way, you will have a more tailored approach.

What should you write to a cold prospect? There are a few simple steps to create the perfect message sequence that will result in a positive engagement rate. We've developed a copy creation framework, called the Honeycomb Creation Framework for crafting outreach messages:

HONEYCOMB CREATION FRAMEWORK
FOR CRAFTING MESSAGES

Target audience

Define your goal

Message strategy

Message crafting

1. **Target audience:** We covered this in Chapter 1 on the ICP, when we looked at the conversation starters and pain points. You will use these to increase the conversion rate.

2. **Define your goal:** Again, the goal here is not to close clients; that is the overall goal of the entire outreach campaign, but not of this sequence of messages. The main goal now is to inspire as many responses as possible, moving into conversations with the cold prospects.

3. **Message strategy:** Review the existing marketing assets that are available to you and how you will approach the target – channels, the number of messages needed in the sequence and the purpose of each message.

4. **Message crafting:** Writing your messages in a style that matches the channel: informal for LinkedIn, formal for email.

Define your goal – what do you want to achieve?

You need a goal – a purpose for reaching out to your cold prospects. A direction in which you want to move the conversation. A journey you want to take your cold prospect on, making them excited and willing to talk to you.

In most cases, the goal is to schedule a call with your cold prospect. That is the case for the majority of our clients – but not all of them.

We have worked with ultra-high-end service providers, in the range of hundreds of thousands of euros, or even millions. This requires a different approach. In this case, our client's goal is not to book a call. We've had clients whose goal was to be invited to play golf or participate in a charity event: an entry point to a place where they could start building the relationship towards a business opportunity.

We all have the urge to jump into a pitch rather than connect with people, but I remember one client who told me: 'You see, in the ultra-high circle of services, it is the people that matter. If you want to sell a service, or set up a partnership in this range, people are looking at *you* – and deciding if they want to do business with you. If yes, then what you have to offer becomes secondary.'

Now let me share a short common scenario, and why it fails to get results.

For the majority of our high-ticket service providers, the goal is to set up a meeting. The standard approach is that the copywriter creates a sequence of messages sent over a period of time, structured as logical steps towards a meeting. And this always fails. It fails because the copywriter is looking at the wrong goal.

A typical sequence of messages is structured as in the image below, with the last message being an invitation for a call or a meeting.

TYPICAL OUTREACH SEQUENCE

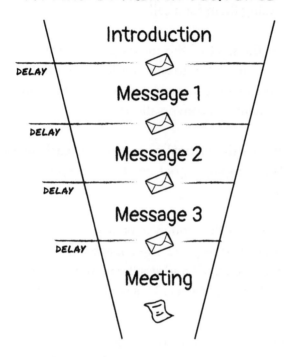

The point of this sequence is to continue reaching out to the prospect, even if they don't respond. If they don't respond to the first message, they will get the second message, then the third and so on. Even if they don't ever engage, they still get the next message.

Now let me ask you: if someone ignores your first, second and third messages, what are the chances that they will jump to book a call when they receive your invitation in the fourth message? Very low, I would say. If they ignored three messages, it means they did not engage with your messages and there is no point even asking them for a call.

What if the goal of the message sequence is just to get a response? Not to sell, not to pitch, not to invite the cold prospect to a meeting or call, but simply to engage them in a conversation?

And this is the critical aspect of outreach messaging. The campaign goal needs to be split into two stages:

1. The goal of the sequence messages is to get prospects to respond and engage with your messages, which address the pain points of your target audience. This is one-to-many communication.

2. Next, the goal of the campaign: to get the prospects who have responded on a call. This is achieved through nurture: one-to-one conversation, where you can set up some flow, but you can't use templates. You are talking to that particular person, from that particular company. I will explain in more detail in Chapter 5 on Nurture.

For now, have a look at the framework below. Based on the ICP, you need to create hooks (conversation starters), with a main goal of passing the response obstacle, getting people to engage with you and starting a conversation. What type of message sequence will encourage your target to respond?

You still have the goal to set up a meeting in mind, but you know that it is further down the campaign.

CONVERSATION SEQUENCE

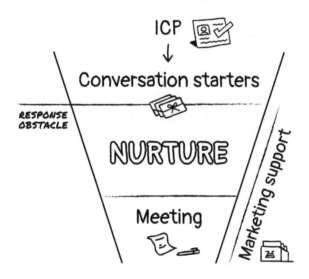

Shifting your goal from a campaign goal towards a message sequence goal is a game changer. Now the copywriter can focus on the content: a message strategy with several conversation starters, increasing the chances that several prospects will engage.

Create the right message strategy

You know the target and the goal. Now you start strategising on how best to create the message sequence.

The first step is to decide how many messages to send. The question is not how many messages you need to send to get a response, but how many different conversation starters can you set up, while avoiding pitching? A sales pitch (soft or hard) is not a conversation starter.

Earlier in Chapter 1: ICP, we discussed pain points and conversation starters. Each message should approach from a different angle. Some prospects will be inspired to respond on the first message, others on the second or third – several messages increase the response rate.

At BizzBee we recommend sending three or four conversation starters. If you do not get a response from any of them, go back to the drawing board. Either your target is not right (they have nothing to do with what you want to talk about) or your message sequence is not talking about the right things.

Don't be tempted to use more than four conversation starters. Stick to three or four.

BizzBee's message structure

You know what you want to communicate (the conversation starter), but you need to clarify how you intend to do so. You also need to consider the delay between the messages. Too short a delay might be perceived as pushy, but if the gap is too long the prospect might lose interest.

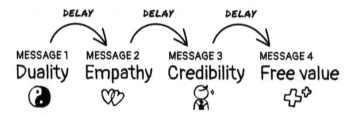

After experimenting with different approaches Bizz-Bee arrived at this four-step structure, which we use for LinkedIn. Using these four messages always gets a fantastic response. But it will only work if your business has a digital aspect, and the needed social proof.

Message 1: Duality

The first conversation starter asks the recipient to choose between two things.

There is something compelling about an either/or choice. I still recall the movie *The Matrix*, where Neo has to choose between a red pill (experiencing reality with all its uncertainties) and a blue pill (living in blissful ignorance in the Matrix world).

If you give your prospects a clear choice between two extremes, our experience has shown you are at least ten times more likely to get a response. People are opinionated by nature; they know what they would choose and they will want to tell you. I am amazed by human nature and how many people respond to duality.

Message 2: Empathy

If the cold prospect ignored your first message, try to show that you understand them and the problems they are facing from a different angle. And if you have done your work on your ICP, you will include the right pain points and get responses. If people like sharing their opinions, they like complaining even more.

Message 3: Credibility

The third message structure is intended to build your credibility. If you failed to engage the cold prospect with your duality and empathy messages, perhaps they do not believe you know enough about the subject to be worth engaging with.

In this message you need to introduce yourself and your business, and position yourself as an expert in the field. We've often found that prospects who ignore the first two conversation starters respond to the credibility message, and engage in conversation.

Message 4: Free value

If someone ignores your first three messages, consider giving them something for free that will help them but will also increase your authority and credibility.

Don't be scared of the 'free' concept. You are just using it to get in the door. We are all used to being sold things through LinkedIn and email. It is refreshing when someone approaches you with something of value for free. It can be the start of a great relationship.

It can be an e-book, article, white paper or anything that is targeted to your ICP. Here are a few ideas from real examples that we have used to approach cold leads:

- **Free e-book:** This is probably the most commonly used free incentive. There is a one-off effort and cost to develop and design the e-book and zero additional effort required to reproduce it. If the topic you address is crucial to the prospects, it could bring enormous value to them. I personally believe this is a great way to get to your prospects, and if the e-book reaches them that means you have their email and can follow up with more messages.

- **Free sample:** Try-before-you-buy is another concept that has been proven successful. The purpose of the free sample is to show your prospects the quality they can expect. And this can work only if their involvement is minimal. For example, at BizzBee we offer a free sample database of ten cold prospects, giving our prospects the opportunity to experience our database-building service.

- **Free demo:** Demos can vary from a video that they can watch at their convenience and their own pace, to a real-time demo over a call. This works quite well in the software industry, where you can showcase some limited features or offer a peek inside. A real-time demo requires more effort from the prospects, however, so I would recommend you avoid it.

- **Free trial:** Famous among SaaS, or digital service providers. You provide your prospects with the full value over a limited time, so they experience your solution. If they find it valuable, they will keep using it and pay for it. If they don't, then there is no point in pushing them further. When we launched HireZZack.com (a mobile and software development prospecting solution), we included an offer of a seven-day free trial during which companies receive free leads for mobile, web and software development. After the seventh day, they need to pay.

- **Free courses:** These provide a two-way benefit. Prospects learn something for free and you demonstrate your credibility and authority. Even if they are not ready to move up the value ladder yet, you position yourself as an expert in the field for the moment when they are ready. At BizzBee, for example, we give away a five-day lead generation course.

- **Free consultation hour:** For most businesses it is too early to introduce this offer for reasons I explain below, but one of our clients used it successfully: an Australian leadership guru who worked with 150 of the Fortune 500 companies and has a published book. Approaching specific positions within corporations, he offered them a one-hour free discussion about their leadership issues, which was a great hit because his credibility ensured that the value was too big to miss. We also use free consultation hours in BizzBee, but as the last step in our marketing campaign where sales take over.

- **Free physical book:** If you truly want to give high value, then a physical book is the best option. It is quite an expensive process (just think about the time it takes to write it), and not many companies do it. Another concept here is free-plus-shipping, where you give away the book for free and charge for the shipping costs (usually €10–20).

- **Other free stuff:** There is no limit to what you can offer for free. You can create relevant blog posts, a set of podcasts, even a compilation of content that was not made by you (eg 'I've spent five years searching and listening to the best mobile development podcasts, and I have created the top ten must-hear podcasts for you'). Just make sure that it is relevant to your target.

These are only a few of the offers you can give to your cold prospects to initiate communication. And you really need to be focused on giving them value, not on bringing them to a landing page and taking their email.

When choosing what kind of free value to offer, keep three main things in mind:

1. The offer that brings the most value to your prospects: You are giving them an 'ethical bribe', something of value, without expecting anything in return.

If you have identified a few things that will be valuable to your target, that you can give for free, look at the one that is most attractive. Cold prospects want to receive a quick fix to some of their problems: a free trial, a free sample, a sneak peek behind the scenes.

Remember that you are reaching out to a cold prospect who has never heard about you and has ignored your previous messages. You have one final small window to capture their attention.

2. The offer that requires minimum effort from your prospects: Your offer might be attractive, but if the prospect has to fill in a long questionnaire, set up an account or talk to you, they might not be willing to make the effort – especially at the beginning, since they don't know you. You can ask for that kind of effort down the road as you build rapport and a relationship.

We've worked with a lot of clients who believe a one-hour free consultation is a great offer. It is presented as having huge value; they get to talk to you for one hour for free. We do have some successful cases but, generally, strangers are not ready to dedicate one hour of their time to you, especially if they are not aware of your credibility. And not everyone is ready to talk to strangers.

I would avoid making this offer, at least at this early stage, when you are simply trying to engage in conversation. Save it for further down the road, when the prospect is engaged and interested in hearing more. A free discovery call, or free consultation call, can be useful as a last push towards setting up a meeting. By then they are not talking to strangers, but friends they've met online.

Even if you have something valuable to share – a free three-day course, say – bear in mind that you are asking for a cold prospect to spend three days of their time listening to you.

In the beginning, the most you can ask of a cold prospect is to confirm that they want the free value, to share a piece of simple information (who in their company is responsible for marketing or website maintenance?), or a simple opinion from them about a topic, nothing more. To the prospect, you are like the person offering samples in the supermarket. 'Try this new brand of cheese.' That's nice enough but they're not going to make any more effort at this stage than taking the cheese that's in front of them. Once they start responding, you can increase the amount of effort required of them.

3. The offer that requires minimum effort from you to provide: Imagine offering something that takes you two or three hours to do. That could be quite valuable – but imagine you need to give it to thirty or fifty prospects per week, for free? I would not make that commitment with cold leads: I would increase my effort when I know the lead is really interested in my services.

We do have examples where we spend two or three hours or even more, but never for cold prospects. In most cases, we have a meeting, understand the scope of the project and, if we want to prove our expertise, we dedicate a few hours to doing a small sample, so the prospect can experience the service before buying. But that is never at the beginning of a relationship.

So, back to you. What is the most attractive thing your business can offer that requires minimum effort on your part? Something that simultaneously brings the most value to your target audience and requires minimum effort from them?

The ZZ outreach channels

What is the best way to reach out to a prospect? Or consider it from another perspective – how would you prefer to be reached? We all have a preferred way of communication. Some people prefer email, whereas others rarely catch up with emails. They might engage with a LinkedIn message from their phone, while others rarely check LinkedIn. Be bold and try different channels – reach prospects on their preferred channel, rather than making them to come to yours (which means extra effort for them).

We have found that email and LinkedIn bring in the best results from B2B prospecting. Both are written mediums that give the prospects the flexibility and opportunity to respond at their convenience. They are nonintrusive, leaving it up to the prospect whether they want to connect. Cold calling is also a possible channel, but I never like it when someone cold calls me. I might be in the middle of another call, or having lunch. The caller requires my full attention, which I am not ready to give to someone I don't know. Perhaps down the road, when I am more confident that it is worth my time, I might be willing to take a call or even make the call myself.

In the beginning, therefore, start with one channel. If the prospect doesn't respond, then move to another, and continue the conversation on the channel that they respond to – because it is the most convenient for them.

Depending on the target, industry and campaign goal, you have to choose how to create synergy between these two channels. One approach is to send LinkedIn invitations first. As you progress through the campaign, you continue conversations with those who respond on LinkedIn. For those who do not respond on LinkedIn, you can create a second-tier sequence via email.

Or you can start with an email campaign and move to LinkedIn for those who don't respond.

A third approach is to start using both channels at the same time. If you do this, you need to set up the messages to be: (a) complementary on both channels, but (b) still stand alone, in case someone sees only the LinkedIn messages or only the emails.

COORDINATING COMMUNICATION CHANNELS

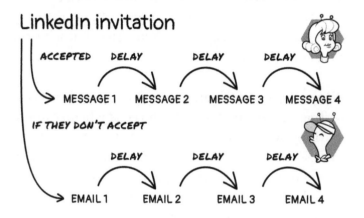

LinkedIn invitation

ACCEPTED DELAY DELAY DELAY

MESSAGE 1 MESSAGE 2 MESSAGE 3 MESSAGE 4

IF THEY DON'T ACCEPT

DELAY DELAY DELAY

EMAIL 1 EMAIL 2 EMAIL 3 EMAIL 4

Craft the messages

After all the planning and decision-making, you can now focus on the actual message writing. There is a science behind knowing what to write and at what point. Over the years, I have conducted outreach for hundreds of clients, closely measuring which kinds of messages work and which don't. I have seen us triple our results by simply changing our copy, so a good outreach copy plan is worth your attention.

Our outreach sequence is usually between three and five messages long, with each email or LinkedIn contact bringing the cold prospect closer to you.

What is the style of writing? Define the style based on your target, not yourself. If you are reaching out to C-level executives, your approach should be more formal. If you are reaching out to start-ups, the style can be informal. Keep your own voice, but adjust it based on who you are writing to.

Where is your ideal target from? This also affects the writing of the message. One choice is whether to use UK English or US English. Or whether to use more sophisticated English words (English-native target) or more conversational English words (non-native English target). You don't want to fail a campaign just because your target can't understand you.

Which channel is the message for? LinkedIn and email need different approaches. In an email, you have a formal introduction, the body of the message and a farewell line followed by a signature. On LinkedIn, you can have an open chat conversation where you don't need an introduction or a signature. And this makes a huge difference.

If you start sending messages on LinkedIn that were written for email, you won't get a significant response rate. LinkedIn is a network where business people chat. So before sending a message, consider whether you would send that kind of message to a friend, supplier or an existing client.

I've seen a million email sequence examples, and I can bet that you have as well. However, when it comes to LinkedIn, there are few good examples available.

Here, I share our ultimate LinkedIn sequence with you. We've spent years perfecting it, and we made a lot of mistakes to get here. Pay attention to the structure of the messages and link usage (or link absence, as we don't use them in our early messages), as well as the tone of the conversation.

LinkedIn sequence sample

The first obstacle on LinkedIn, before you even consider sending the conversation starter sequence, is to get your invitation to connect accepted.

Sending connection requests

I've experienced bad examples of requests, where the invitation message includes a full pitch. I don't connect with people who do that. They are intruding in my space, without even asking my permission.

Each message in your sequence has one specific goal, and the goal of the invitation message is to simply get connected. Not to introduce yourself, not to try to sell a product – but to just simply get connected. You will have plenty of opportunities down the road to pitch if your invitation is accepted, but if it isn't accepted, you won't, so focus on that. Here are a few examples of how simple your invitation message should be:

Hi [first name]. Your profile is very impressive. I would be glad to connect.

Hi [first name]. It seems like we share similar interests. Let's connect.

Hi [first name], let's connect.

I know plenty of people think you should state your intent in the invitation message. I say you don't. Your goal is to connect with the person and build a relationship. If they state right away that they have a problem and need help, of course you can follow up on that. But otherwise, you are here to nurture a long-term relationship.

Recently, I checked my LinkedIn profile and I had 355 pending invitations. Only thirty had a customised message. All of them were pitching something directly in the invitation message. I would rather accept people without anything in the invitation message, than people who send a pitch. I tested that, and other people felt the same.

To increase your acceptance rate, your connection requests need to be more personalised. Perhaps you share a contact, you are in the same LinkedIn group or you like the same LinkedIn page. Look at the person's latest post and mention it in the connection request.

If you prefer quality over quantity, personalisation always helps, but it takes additional time.

And this has to be done every day. Consistency is the key. If you send 20 invitations to your ideal targets daily, that means 100 invitations per week, 400 invitations per month or 4,800 invitations per year. And if you have a good acceptance rate, of let's say 50%, you are looking at 2,400 new connections a year. And all these have the potential to become your client because **they fit your ICP.**

Sending the follow-up sequence

If a highly targeted person accepts your connection request, you are one step closer. It means that now you have access to their posts and their problems and you can directly message them without any additional costs.

When the main goal of your follow-up sequence is receiving a response, usually the messages are tailored towards conversation rather than a pitch.

The example below shows a sequence of messages that I made targeting sales and business development decision-makers in management consultancies with 50–200 employees. I ran it on five profiles, covering different geographical areas: UK, Germany, Austria, Benelux, Nordic, Switzerland and France.

We created five messages, using automation for the LinkedIn outreach so they are slightly generic, trying to feel personal. If you are sending follow-ups manually, you have endless opportunities for customisation and personalisation.

We got fantastic results, which is why I want to share the messages and the logic behind each, and dissect the messages to give you the reasoning behind each word.

Message 1: Follow-up (as soon as possible after connection)

The purpose of my first follow-up is to first state the country that we are both from (increase personalisation) and that we are colleagues. Also, 99% of people making these contacts (at least the ones who did not pitch in the invitation) will use the first follow-up to pitch, without knowing anything about the prospect. By not doing that, I will stand out.

> 'Thanks for allowing me to be part of your network. I am happy to connect with fellow consultants from [country].'

'Part of your network' – I am joining their network, not welcoming them to my network. This gives them the perception that I appreciate being part of their network. 'I am happy' – makes me a human with emotions, and not just an automated text. 'Connect with fellow consultants' – sets the tone of a dialogue between friends and collaborators, rather than with a supplier (an important distinction). 'Country' – adds to the feeling that a human is writing the message.

Message 2: Follow-up (one day after previous message)

The goal of this second message is to create **duality** and try to prompt the prospect to make a choice with a statement that they can either agree or disagree with. Or perhaps they will not think it is relevant to them. But in all three cases they will feel the urge to reply. Which is my main goal – to start a conversation.

> 'By the way, how are things in [country]? I had a chat with a few consultants, and opinions seem divided. On the one hand, it's up to us to help companies survive this crisis, while on the other hand, their budget is getting tighter. I would love to hear your opinion on this.'

'By the way' demonstrates the 'human' approach, rare in automation. 'How are things in [country]?' – I don't want to get into a deep conversation from the start. It's a surface-level conversation starter, just to get a response. 'I had a chat with a few consultants, and opinions seem divided' – so it is not just a thought from me, but after talking to a few colleagues, I became aware of these divided opinions. 'On the one hand' vs 'on the other hand' is not presenting the options as good or bad, and there is no right answer, it is just a choice – but it requires an answer. 'Love to hear your opinion' is a call to action (CTA) to respond with a personal touch.

This kind of message gets a pretty high response. Do I then respond suggesting a meeting? Of course not. I'm just at the start of a relationship.

You can even prepare a chess map of potential responses and how to handle them. Not exact quotes, but flow charts on how to drive the conversation if they agree or disagree with your question. If they **disagree** (budgets are not tighter or it is not up to consultants) my message has engaged them – good. Now I need to follow up with an open-ended question to encourage them to keep responding and messaging. 'How do you mean?', or 'Why do you think that?', or 'Interesting… can you elaborate?' They will respond in more detail and I will see how to progress the conversation. If they **agree** (budgets are tighter and it is up to consultants), again, good, I got a response.

But don't try to cover all the answers you might get at this stage. That is part of the nurture stage, see Chapter 5.

Message 3: Follow-up (three days after previous message)
The goal here is to show **empathy**, that I understand the prospect and the kind of problems they are facing. But I also ask how they reach out to clients – which is a hook towards our service.

'I had a thought I wanted to share. If our job is to help companies, what can we do to get our voice heard by as many companies as possible? I mean, the B2B segment usually involves a longer sales cycle, there are multiple people involved and it is not always a simple process. And Facebook ads are not really meant to help us in the B2B world. So, are you successfully reaching out to business? Is your voice heard?'

'I had a thought' – again, this is a human approach (a person is sharing a thought). 'What can we do to get our voice heard by as many companies as possible?' – I could have just said advertising, marketing or promotion. But the more fancy keywords we use, the more sophisticated the message sounds, the more likely it is to seem like an automated message. And this particular question opens the door for what they can do in marketing. 'I mean' is another human aspect. 'The B2B... longer sales cycle... multiple people involved... not a simple process' – I am showing empathy, understanding their problem. The more accurately you reflect the problem, the better you will connect with prospects. And I add B2B here to ensure I am talking to the right audience.

This type of message also brings a lot of conversions. Prospects feel that you understand them, and are keen to engage in conversation.

Some of them will say they are doing a lot, opening the door for follow-up questions. In order of priority (you do not need to ask all these questions), I would ask: 'What are you doing?', 'Is it working?', 'Are you happy with the results?', 'Have you heard about alternatives?', 'Do you do cold prospecting?' If they do, 'Have you considered outsourcing it?' The goal is to understand what point they are at at the moment, but this exchange is part of the nurture process. If they are not doing a lot – there are still follow-up questions like 'Why not?', 'Do you think you should?', 'What is stopping you from reaching out to many more companies?' These are the type of open questions that could keep the prospect talking and provide you with more insights.

And as you engage with the prospects, don't make it an interview or a monologue. Try to share some personal experience yourself to make sure it is a conversation.

Message 4: Follow-up (two days after previous message)

This message is for people who received the duality message and did not respond, then received the empathy message and still did not respond. This probably means that they do not think I am worthy of a response. The goal of this fourth message is to boost my **credibility** and give background on my business:

'Sorry, I jumped into questions without properly introducing myself. I work at BizzBee Solutions, a business consulting company that actively helps B2B service providers reach out to as many companies as possible with zero spend on ads.

I am a certified management consultant (CMC), I have an MSc in entrepreneurship and executive MBA in management (Sheffield University).

BizzBee Solutions has helped more than 400 companies in reaching out to their ideal targets, building relationships and scheduling warm meetings with their prospective clients. Our outreach is based on LinkedIn, and it works.

I have worked with plenty of consultants and high-ticket service providers in general. If interested, I can name a few clients from [country] that we've managed to help and the results we achieved.'

'Sorry' – again I start with a human approach. 'I work at BizzBee Solutions...' is a one-sentence explainer of the value that my company provides. 'I am a...' feels a bit too much, but because I am approaching management consultants with 50–200 employees, I need to prove I am worth their time. Although I have plenty of certificates, certified management consultant (CMC) is the most relevant. The MSc in entrepreneurship and EMBA in management also boost my credibility, showing that I am not a newbie. 'BizzBee has helped...' is a one-paragraph credibility-builder for the company, because I am trying to bring new business for the company, not for me. 'I have worked with plenty of consultants...' – explicitly stating that I have helped other consultants like them, so I know what I am doing. 'If interested, I can name a few clients from [country]...' – I'm showing I have already worked with other consultants from that country, but I don't attach links or provide quotes from testimonials or case studies. I want to obtain their permission – because this is the fourth message – and I want to get them responding.

My numbers show quite a lot of responses after this message. Once people see that I have authority, they are keener to engage in a conversation. If they are **interested**, I have country-specific case studies and examples that I can show to them to improve our credibility in working with consultants. If they are **not interested**, I remember that they actually made the effort to respond. That is better than being ignored. A simple 'Why not?' is a great conversation starter to try to bring them back into conversation. But don't be too pushy – you want a relationship, not to irritate your potential clients.

Message 5: Follow-up (three days after previous message)

The most common mistake I see in automation sequences is that people add an invitation to schedule a call in the last message. And I understand the temptation – you have made a significant effort, and this is your last hope to get an appointment. But try to look at this from the prospect's point of view. They have ignored four messages. Do you think they will suddenly want a meeting? Of course not. Avoid embarrassment, and instead try to give them **free value**.

> 'I guess you are probably on holiday. So I should probably stop before I start annoy-ing you. I wanted to get in touch to exchange thoughts on what is happening at the moment and how, as consultants, we can help.
>
> I also wanted to share an e-book we've devel-oped to help B2B service providers reach out to more companies and convert them to clients – all through LinkedIn. I believe you will find it insightful, as it is based on all the mistakes and lessons learned so far. And there were a lot…
>
> Would you like a copy of the e-book?'

'I guess you are probably on holiday' – I am trying to justify their action to ignore me. 'stop… annoying you' – a human recognition that I may be overdoing it. 'I wanted to…' is making a statement on my purpose in messaging – building a relationship, exchanging thoughts. 'I also wanted to share an e-book…' – I'm giving them a free e-book, but I don't want to add the overused keyword FREE. 'It is based on all the mistakes and lessons learned so far' – I add weight and value to the e-book. It is not just a how-to, but rather insights learned from mistakes. 'Would you like a copy of the e-book?' – as you can see, I never send a link without their permission.

If they have accepted your connection invitation, but have not responded to four messages, it means that they are not interested. Politely move them out of the sequence, but leave the door open by sharing relevant content on your profile to remind them about you.

In some cases, you could also consider sending an additional message, but it should be purpose-driven. For example, if you are doing a webinar on a subject relevant to them, you might want to personally invite them.

Chapter takeaway

Creating B2B outreach messages – crafting messages that will motivate cold prospects to respond and engage in conversation – is an art.

Knowing the ICP and the conversation topic is a starting point. You must know who you are writing to.

Next you need to **define your goal**. You must differentiate between campaign goal and message sequence goal. They are two completely different goals. Focus on the message sequence goal: to get a response.

Then you need to set the **message strategy**. Define how many messages you need. Each message should address a different pain point and act as a different conversation starter. Define the structure of each message, especially what free value you will give in the last message. Have in mind how much effort is involved in your free value for your prospect, and for yourself. Then you need to define through which channels you want to approach, and in what order.

Finally, you can start crafting messages. Have in mind different writing styles. Make your messages more formal or informal depending on your target and adjust your messages depending on your geographic reach. Finally, you need to adjust the messages for LinkedIn and email.

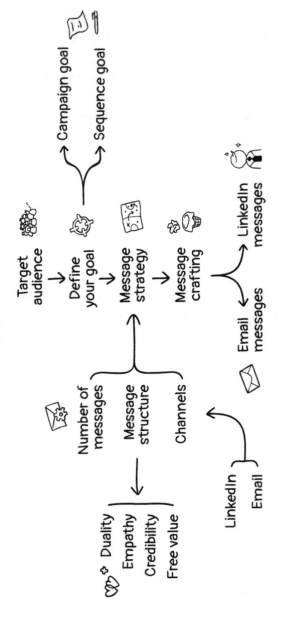

HONEYCOMB CREATION FRAMEWORK
FOR CRAFTING MESSAGES

Target audience → Define your goal → Message strategy → Message crafting

Define your goal → Campaign goal
Define your goal → Sequence goal

Message strategy → Number of messages / Message structure / Channels

Message structure → Duality / Empathy / Credibility / Free value

Channels → LinkedIn / Email

Message crafting → LinkedIn messages
Message crafting → Email messages

Part 1: Conclusion

Once you have reached the end of Part 1, the hardest part of the ZZ Framework is complete. Seriously.

I recall a less widely known quote from the entrepreneurship coach Brian Tracy: 'Every minute you spend in planning saves 10 minutes in execution; this gives you a 1,000 percent return on energy.'[8] And I truly believe that.

A well-made plan, and good preparation, will save a lot of headaches. For me, a well-made plan is not a plan that has covered every single detail. Such a plan leaves no flexibility for adjustments during execution

---

8   B Tracy, *Mastering Your Time* (Jaico Publishing House, 1998)

when you receive market feedback. I live and breathe agile project management. For me a well-made plan is a plan that has established a great framework within which the execution can prosper. As such, the execution can add value on top of the framework and be easily updated to absorb feedback from the market.

But enough about planning. The time is ripe to start making honey for your business, and the next section will tell you how to execute your campaign.

SECTION TWO
DIGITAL OUTREACH EXECUTION

4

Campaign Execution (Honey Production)

The execution framework

Back to our bee story – it can't be all fun in flower-beds and happy hive-building, right? After the planning phase, the bees need to roll up their sleeves or empty their sacs. They've collected all that nectar to produce some sweet honey. So how do they do that? As you might imagine, it's an exhausting, multistep process. The hive is always busy. The house bees wait for the foragers to return. The worker bees pass the nectar to the waiting bees so the honey-making can start.

Even with all these bees involved, the job is not done yet. The nectar still contains too much water, even though some has been removed, so the bees have to keep working to dry it out and improve quality. There are two methods that they use.

Firstly, they spread the honey over the honeycomb to increase the surface area so the water can evaporate faster, and they also fan their wings near the honey to increase airflow, evaporating even more liquid.

Before they can make honey, they work to reduce the water content from 70% to about 17–20%. That's what I call results!

Our outreach also has two methods: reaching out via email and via LinkedIn.

This chapter covers the first steps in execution that lead to pushing the 'start' button. (In the next chapter we cover how to deal with responses and how to report on your results.) We established that I am a strong believer in text-based outreach and that LinkedIn and email are the best channels for B2B text-based outreach. There are two ways to proceed with email and LinkedIn execution: manual or automatic.

Manual execution might seem outdated but we recommend it for small and narrow target audiences. For example, a property development company from Ibiza came to us looking for potential private and corporate investors from Spain, Luxembourg, Monaco, Switzerland and the UK. Not surprisingly, there were only a few hundred in total.

In a case like this, you can manually customise and per-
sonalise each message both on email and on LinkedIn.
With only a few hundred prospects you can't afford to do
A/B testing or use a more generic automated approach.

In most other cases, automation is the best way. Bizz-
Bee Solutions prefers to use automation tools in order
to be able to help more clients. There are many automation tools, and new ones emerge all the time. They
save you a huge amount of time and provide you with
complete reporting so you can understand how to
improve your campaigns.

EXTRA HONEY: EMAIL AUTOMATION TOOLS

We do extensive research on all the campaign automation
tools, comparing pricing, features and pros and cons,
which we update frequently. We've made separate sheets
for email automation tools and LinkedIn automation tools:
www.BizzBeeSolutions.com/book-resources.

Automation is growing towards merging email and
LinkedIn outreach in a single automation tool, giving
you a cohesive multichannel approach.

What I really like about this kind of automation is that it
adds extra steps in the outreach process. You can automatically interact with your prospect's LinkedIn profile.
For example, you automatically visit the profile (it will
show up in their notifications) and like or comment on

a few of their posts, so when you invite them to connect you are not a stranger. It hardly matters which automation tool you use – all of them follow the same concept: you configure the tool, set up the message sequence and database, and launch the campaign.

Keeping the bee analogy, we've named our Honey Production Framework for Campaign Execution. The diagram below shows both email and LinkedIn execution.

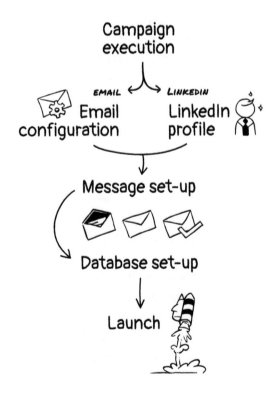

HONEY PRODUCTION FRAMEWORK
FOR CAMPAIGN EXECUTION

Our Honey Production framework is almost the same for email and LinkedIn outreach, with just one different first step for each.

1. **Email configuration (specific to email outreach):** Creating a fresh new email address for the campaign, warming up the new email (over several weeks) and configuring it to the email automation tool you are using.

2. **Strong LinkedIn profile (specific to LinkedIn outreach):** An outdated or CV-like profile will not yield results, however much effort you put in. Your profile needs to have a funnel quality. If you get it right it will attract a lot of prospects and even show in LinkedIn search results.

3. **Message set-up:** The next step is to configure the sequence you built in the previous chapter and set up the message sequence, delays, etc.

4. **Database set-up:** After the sequence is set, you need to upload the database you've built, ensuring that the automation understands the columns and is ready to use the email column.

Email configuration

First, decide on an email address that you will send the email campaign from. I would not recommend using your business email. When I was new to cold outreach, I started my first outreach campaign from my business email. I can still vividly remember how, as we were progressing with the campaign, I received complaints that even my regular emails were ending up in spam. It took me months to restore my email to normal.

These are your three next steps:

1. Create a new email address
2. Warm up the email address
3. Configure the automation

One option is to just create a new email address. If your company's policy is name.surname@domain.com, then just create a new email with name@domain.com, but don't use a generic email for the campaign (eg sales@domain.com, marketing@domain.com, etc).

Another option is to buy a completely new domain with just a small variation from your main domain, and use that for email campaigns. This way, you would be less concerned about the domain spam score, which can affect the overall business messaging.

In both cases, warm up your new email by sending manual emails. Email your friends, family and colleagues. Make sure you get replies and build a conversation. Send ten to twenty emails per day, for the first few weeks. This will significantly improve your deliverability rate.

Next, configure your email address on the email automation tool you want to use. In most cases, you get questions like email, credentials and IMAP/ SMTP information. These SMTP settings (sending emails) and IMAP settings (receiving emails) are just a way of telling the email automation tool how to connect to your email provider. In most cases, this is where you access your regular business email (probably where you host your website or where you bought your domain). Send a test email to check the connection.

Some automation tools offer their own email server (eg Mailchimp), but they are more focused on inbound subscribers (people who left their email on your website) and rarely allow cold outreach.

The set-up process sounds technical but is quite easy. However, there is a lot that can go wrong so we have developed a few configuration tests.

Pre-test: Check your email server limitations. Even if you have bought a campaign automation tool with bigger capacity, if your email server has a smaller capacity you won't be able to use all your automation capacity. If your new outreach automation tool allows you to send 2,000 emails per day, but your email server has a 500 emails per day limit, then you will only be allowed to send 500 emails a day.

Test 1: Log into your email account (via Outlook or the web). If you've just created a new email for the campaign, first ensure it works properly. Manually access the email to ensure that the username and password exist.

Test 2: Send and receive an email, manually, to verify that your new email address works.

Tests 3 and 4: Send a single email via your email automation tool and respond. This will tell you if the email automation tool is capable of sending and receiving emails. If this works, send an email to three people at once, to test the multiple sending functionality.

Test 5: Send a two-email sequence to yourself and reply to those emails. With this test, you are actually testing the drip functionality (and delays), and making sure that it can handle the sequencing. If it works, the next step is to send an email drip to between three and six people to verify that it handles bulk sequencing properly.

Once all these tests are completed, then you have successfully configured your email and can be confident that the campaign won't encounter any problems. If you get stuck at any step, there will be a clear understanding of which part of the automation is not working.

Strong LinkedIn profile

I've seen many clients polishing their LinkedIn profile before considering their ideal client. That is the wrong way around. How can you tailor your profile if you don't know who you are talking to? You will end up with a generic profile that does not resonate with your target. So, first, look again at your ICP, then polish your profile to talk to that specific audience.

Ensure that your profile is strong before even considering reaching out to people. The foundation of all LinkedIn effort is focused on a person. And that person's profile should have a clear message – a synergy between the photo, the experience and the about section.

Most people set up their profile in a CV-like format – which is boring. Look at your profile as one of your marketing/sales funnels. Think of it as a shop window. It represents the personal brand of you, as well as representing the company's brand. A properly set up LinkedIn profile can give you an SEO boost. It can position your profile first in the search results, as well as attract your ideal client. This means you will attract more customers to your business. Our team has spent significant time testing and figuring out the best way to set up a LinkedIn profile that brings customers in. But, again, first be clear who you are talking to.

For example, if you want to target SaaS companies your profile should (within five to ten seconds) show a SaaS person that you are relevant and worth connecting with. The profile's emphasis should be on how you can help SaaS companies improve their subscription rates or reduce churn rates – terms that are crucial for a SaaS target.

Having a strong LinkedIn profile affects the acceptance rate, response rate and even the conversion rate. It's obvious that the most effective LinkedIn profiles are those that are complete. A profile that's missing important information makes the reader wonder if you're hiding something or if you don't take your brand seriously. Taking the time to fill in all the sections proves that you are thorough and have good follow-through.

Here are the most common (and obvious) aspects people overlook.

Profile and cover photo

It goes without saying that your photo needs to be professional and approachable. LinkedIn profiles with professional headshots get fourteen times more profile views.[9] If you haven't done a professional photoshoot

---

9   J Nemo, 'How to Make Your LinkedIn Profile 20x More Appealing, According to Science', Inc., 2017, www.inc.com/john-nemo/how-to-make-your-linkedin-profile-20x-more-appealing-according-to-science.html

for LinkedIn, consider doing this. Choose a photo in which you look genuinely happy, with a warm engaging smile. It should be a good quality photo of you (not a group photo), facing forward so you are 'looking into the eyes' of those who are evaluating you. Your LinkedIn profile is 40% more likely to be clicked on if it contains a photo.[10] Remember, this picture is often the first time a prospect will see your face. Make sure it gives the right first impression.

Profile summary

This is where you really sell yourself to potential connections. Your summary should expand on what appears in your headline, highlighting your specialisms, career experience, noteworthy accolades and thought leadership. It should briefly summarise what your company does and how it helps your clients. It should also show the passion behind your work. You can expand on your role and functions within the company or your core product and service. Beware of delivering a full sales pitch in your summary. It is your chance to tell your own story, so don't use it to simply list your skills or the jobs you've had. Try to bring to life the importance of those skills and how you can help your target audience. The summary requires a significant time investment because it's your most personal piece of content marketing, and it's worth

---

10 A Augustine, 'Ask Amanda: What Should My LinkedIn Profile Photo Look Like?', TopResume, no date, www.topresume.com/career-advice/how-to-pick-perfect-linkedin-profile-photo

the effort. This is your chance to showcase your personality and authenticity, so make the most of it.

Your opening sentence can be a question. It should be positive or provocative enough to keep the reader interested in learning more. I'm sure you've heard it before, but the only goal of the first sentence is to make the reader want to read the second sentence. And so on and so on. So make your summary easily readable but also attractive to your target. You can always do that by sharing your personal history in business. And always make sure that you put a CTA at the end. Even though you are doing outreach, there is no reason not to try to initiate some action on their part. Decide what you want to accomplish and make sure that the reader knows as well. Should they contact you via LinkedIn or via email, or maybe they should simply pick up the phone? Always communicate the next step clearly.

Relevant content

The importance of visual content is constantly growing, so if you have relevant videos, presentations or infographics make sure you include them on your profile. But the written word is still appreciated, so use it to your advantage. Share a business story or two. Add a dash of personality. Show your prospects that you are a person worth knowing.

If you are new to LinkedIn or don't have any content yet, start by sharing someone else's content. And progress towards sharing your own thoughts and stories. Comment on other people's posts, especially if they are part of your target – everyone wants to receive compliments, and giving them costs nothing.

Recommendations and endorsements

Endorsements give people viewing your profile a quick, visual sense of what you're valued for. Recommendations take this a step further. They are personal testimonials written to provide insight into your professional brands. If you ask people you've worked with, or within your community, you can easily enrich this LinkedIn section.

Experience, education and volunteering

Always choose your employer or educational institution from the LinkedIn list. This will automatically add the appropriate logo to your profile. In addition to the visual appearance, your profile gets an extra dose of credibility, thanks to the brand association. Your employment and volunteer experience sections need to be filled out with your experience professionally or as a volunteer, mentioning relevant achievements and areas of expertise.

Add the experience that complements what you are currently doing. Make sure you highlight the accomplishments and results that you achieved. If you think that it's appropriate, use the job title as a place to add some of the keywords. It won't be possible for every previous job experience, if they are not related to the same field, but you can try to include them.

Skills

Add skills related to the keywords used in the previous sections of the profile. You can add a maximum of fifty, and make sure to add skills that you know you will be endorsed for, and that are relevant to your target and the solution you're trying to sell.

Powerful LinkedIn headline

The headline is where your prospects form part of their first impression and it can be a double-edged sword. You can't go wrong with incorporating your current position, but here comes the tricky part. Should you incorporate a bit more? Well, in most cases, it depends on the target, but also on your solution.

Your headline should grab your reader's attention and compel them to read more, so in some cases, it's useful to clearly state what you do, who you are and what benefit you bring to others. Even in this area, there are two directions – stacking the headline with relevant keywords or crafting it as a statement. I recommend the second option.

Here are a few examples of headlines stacked with keywords:

- Executive Leader • Marketing Strategist • Expert Consultant • CRM & Loyalty • Customer Experience

- Project Manager ▶ Made in NY Campus at Bush Terminal I Quality-obsessed Construction Professional

- Sales Professional ▶ Security Systems Integrator ★ Commercial Solutions I Healthcare I Higher Ed I Hospitality I Retail

On the other hand, here are a few examples of what a statement headline should look like:

- Here, we put emphasis on the benefit the person provides or how he/she helps people/companies to achieve _____ [insert value]

- Helping Companies Translate Their Business Goals and Ideas into Operational Reality and Positive ROI

- Helping Businesses Develop Strong Sales Forces through Intensive Sales Training Programmes

There is no straightforward formula for whether you should go with a simple headline or add a value proposition or personality. You can always test to see what works best for you and your target audience.

Once your profile is ready, look at the campaign execution. Like email outreach, LinkedIn outreach can be performed manually or automatically depending on your target and the degree of personalisation you want to involve.

In the next section we will focus on automated LinkedIn outreach.

Automated message set-up

Regardless of whether for email or LinkedIn, the automated message set-up follows the same principles.

You need to set up the:

1. Message sequence

2. Delays between messages

3. Time when the messages should be sent

Message sequence: In most automation tools, you are given steps to follow. On email you set up the subject title and the body, whereas LinkedIn only needs the message.

While copying the messages, some automation tools give you an analysis of the message – the length of the subject, word count, question count, reading level, positivity, even counting the number of spam words.

You can use these metrics to predict the overall probability of receiving a response.

When you've finished setting up the messages, set up the **delays** between messages. We usually allow three or four working days' delay between each message. This way, the majority of your prospects won't be annoyed (imagine receiving an email or LinkedIn message every day from someone you don't even know). However, don't let your prospects forget you – if you send them one message a week or a month, their awareness level of your company and solution will drop significantly.

The next step is the **schedule set-up**. Both LinkedIn and email automation tools let you choose what day of the week and time to distribute the messages.

According to a recent study conducted by Adobe,[11] respondents reported spending an average of 209 minutes checking their work email and 143 minutes checking their personal email, for a total of 352 minutes (about five hours and fifty-two minutes) each day. But almost half (48%) of respondents said they don't check their work emails until they start working.

---

11 A Johnson Hess, 'Here's How Many Hours American Workers Spend on Email Each Day', CNBC.com, 2019, www.cnbc.com/2019/09/22/heres-how-many-hours-american-workers-spend-on-email-each-day.html

We set our campaign schedules by the prospect's work day and time zone, setting messages to be sent Monday to Friday, during a nine-to-five working day.

Time zones are an added complication, but you know your ICP so you can afford to spend some time on setting the appropriate sending schedules.

Database set-up

The next step is to add the people you want to reach. The majority of email and LinkedIn automation tools will give you the option to import a CSV (comma-separated values) file.

Ninety-nine percent of the time, we import from CSV because it is a real time-saver (and we already have our databases organised neatly in a spreadsheet). I highly recommend you do the same. If you don't know how, look back at Chapter 2 on the Database.

When you upload the CSV file, map out the attributes – showing the automation tool which column contains the name, surname, position, email, etc. These attributes are actually the personalisation variables. Don't panic if you can't find the one you need in the list. If you had it as a column on the spreadsheet, you can easily add it as a custom field.

If you are not 100% certain of the quality of the database, do check:

- **Contact name:** We tend to keep our outreach casual and friendly, so when speaking to our prospects we use their first names. It's up to you to decide the tone that you will use. Finding your voice is key, but if you also don't like to sound formal then make sure that you are using the prospect's first name. You don't want to use the first name and middle name when the only person who does that is their grandmother (when she's angry).

- **Company name:** Make sure you have the right company name, preferably the one they commonly use. If you built the database using mainly LinkedIn, pay extra attention to this. Some companies put their slogan or description next to their company name, eg Shipley Associates: We Help Companies Win Business; Sense Worldwide: We help people to innovate. Watch out for this – it will look like you didn't bother to check if you use the slogan as the name.

- **Letter case:** As with any part of the copy, make sure that you use appropriate grammar and letter case. Using capital and small letters is fairly easy, but extremely important when it comes to delivering the right message and sounding like a real human being. Avoid using caps lock. You don't want your prospects to think that you are yelling at them.

- **Diacritics:** You know those weird-looking letters? Eg ā, ē, ī, ū, č, ǵ, ķ, ļ, ņ, š, ž, ñ, ä, ö, ø, å, etc. These letters with marks above, below, through or on the letters are rare in English, but common in many other languages. If you are targeting German or Swedish companies then, of course, you can write to them in English, but in personalising the messages you would use their names or company names. And here comes the problem. Most of the automation tools, if not all, don't recognise these letters, so they substitute question marks. Now imagine your name is Björn, and you receive an email that starts Hi Bj?rn. You would probably report it as spam or delete it right away. So be careful of these letters; they require some manual work while importing. Better safe than sorry.

- **Other variables:** Be careful if you are using variables in a sentence – make sure that if the variables being imported are not names (eg references to an industry), the sentence where they are used is grammatically correct. For example, many times when we insert an industry in a sentence, we need to check whether we need 'a' or 'an' before it.

When you are absolutely sure that the prospects list looks perfect, you are ready for the final step. Make sure that you are satisfied with the settings and are ready to launch the campaign.

As stated earlier, you can set up an automated Linked-In-only campaign by just using Sales Navigator (if the industry you want to reach is one of the available filters) and setting up the automation to message your search results. But remember that this short cut means you don't get the other benefits of building your own database, such as qualifying each prospect.

Once you have configured the automation tools and set up the message and the database, you are ready to kick off the campaign, and push the launch button. All your hard work has been leading up to this magical moment. Now you just have to know what to do with the results.

Chapter takeaway

There are some key differences between email and LinkedIn outreach, but a lot of similarities.

For email outreach, you need to **configure your email**. Create a new email address or even a new domain for outreach purposes. You need some warm-up activity for the new email before you increase the quantity of messages. Once the email is ready, connect to an email automation tool and make sure you have the correct configuration.

For LinkedIn outreach, you must have a **strong LinkedIn profile**. Update your profile and cover photo, profile summary, headline and so on, to speak to your ideal target profile.

Set up your automated message: The message sequence, the delays between each messages and the scheduled time of delivery.

Import your database as a CSV. You need to map the attributes to the columns, ensure you have the right fields and check any issues with letter case or diacritics. You might need to do some extra manual work here.

Once all this done, you are ready to launch the outreach campaign.

HONEY PRODUCTION FRAMEWORK
FOR CAMPAIGN EXECUTION

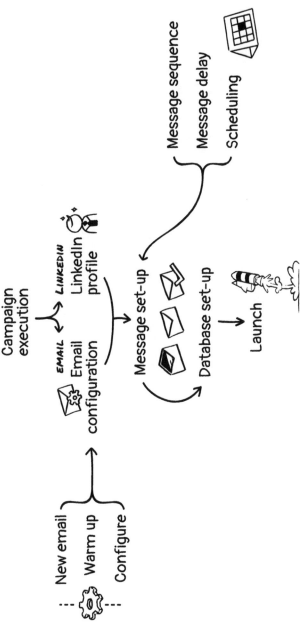

Campaign execution

EMAIL
Email configuration

LINKEDIN
LinkedIn profile

New email
Warm up
Configure

Message set-up

Database set-up

Launch

Message sequence
Message delay
Scheduling

5
Nurture
(Honey Tasting)

The nurture framework

Tastes linger in our memory for such a long time, whether good or bad. When you think of honey, the first thing that comes to mind is probably its rich taste and texture, its divine sweetness. To truly savour the honey, it needs to be harvested.

The bees' last task in the honey production process is capping the honey-filled comb with wax. But to taste the sweet honey, we need to extract it into a jar.

First, we check the frames and make sure that the honeycomb is capped. You don't want to harvest uncapped honey if you can help it; it still has too much moisture in it and might ferment. Then the honeycomb has to be transported from the hive to the place where the honey will be extracted. Next you remove the wax cap that seals in the honey, so it can be extracted. This is a tricky process. The last step is pouring the honey into jars, ready to be tasted.

As you can see, it is an obstacle course from producing the honey to actually tasting it. In the same way we also need to clear a series of obstacles when we undertake an outreach project, before we find some potential clients ready to talk to us.

The nurture stage starts when someone responds to your campaign. Whether you used an automated (one-to-many) or manual approach, once someone responds to a message you need to shift your focus to one-to-one conversation. The primary purpose of the automated campaign is to tempt the ideal client with various hooks and see which results in most conversions. Once someone responds, they are removed from the automated sequence and moved towards manual nurture. This chapter is about the nurturing process: how to move a cold prospect after responding to an automated campaign to scheduling a meeting.

I admit that this is the hardest part of the outreach. Before this point you have control: a pre-planned target, prepared messages and automation tools that you can configure yourself. But now you have to deal with an unpredictable dialogue and reply to the cold prospect's questions and comments. I have seen many outreach campaigns collapse simply from lack of attention to nurture. If you rush the prospect, or offer a solution without first understanding whether they have a problem and what it is, the dialogue is a waste of time – for both of you.

So be like the bees: consider this process as a set of obstacles. You can exchange one message or fifty, but you can't go to the next obstacle until you have overcome the previous one. You can't extract the honey until you have taken the wax cap off. An easy prospect will pass smoothly through the funnel. A challenging prospect will require a lot of guidance. Some prospects will not like the funnel process, and even be offended that you are writing to them.

Throughout the funnel journey, you will receive a lot of rejections. Otherwise, the funnel would be shaped like a rectangle. A 'No' has completely different meanings at different stages of the nurture process. At the beginning, No probably means that the prospect doesn't want to engage in a relationship. On the other hand, a No at the meeting stage means that they are still not convinced that you can help. A negative response needs a different approach at a different stage in the nurture process.

Another way to look at a negative response is to see it as feedback. Someone made the effort to write 'No'. And in sales we love feedback. We love it when someone says Yes, No or Maybe, because that is feedback on how to proceed with that particular lead. The worst is if they ignore your message. Then you have nothing to follow up, because they are not interested in engaging.

Interestingly, the further down the funnel a prospect travels, the easier it is to transform the Nos into Yeses. I will give you some hints on how to handle the answer No at each stage of the nurture process.

Another crucial aspect of the nurturing process is marketing support. How quickly a prospect will move down the funnel depends on the quality of the nurturing process, but the transition will be smoother if you have testimonials, case studies or white papers, or if you are positioned as an expert in the field. So you should keep marketing support in mind when planning an outreach campaign, and that support will be different at each stage of the nurturing process.

Also, keep in mind that LinkedIn responses need to be different from email responses. I explained in the previous chapter why you should keep to a chatty style on LinkedIn, and more formal longer paragraphs on email. Never, I mean never, do it the other way around.

And remember, nurture is human-to-human conversation. It should not be like interviewing people. Try to add some value and personal insight to the conversation. Whatever stage in the funnel the prospect is at, you need to pay attention to your responses.

I suggest a sandwich approach for this. When someone replies to the conversation starter, first try to acknowledge what they've just said, even add some additional information to it. Then you introduce new information and finish with a question. This way, you keep the conversation going and avoid a one-way monologue.

Our nurture framework is called the Honey Tasting Framework for Lead Nurturing, and can help you move cold prospects more easily and quickly down the funnel. It's based on the obstacles that the prospect needs to overcome to agree to a meeting (and therefore the obstacles that you need to overcome).

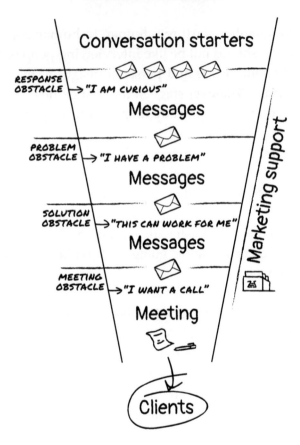

HONEY TASTING FRAMEWORK
FOR LEAD NURTURING

In this section, we will go over each of the obstacles. We'll also cover how you can move prospects down the funnel.

1. **Response obstacle:** If you prepared your cold outreach properly, there is nothing to worry about here. Identifying the right problems for your ideal

client, and ensuring your messages resonate with them, will get plenty of responses.

2. **Problem obstacle:** Many respondents will get stuck here. You cannot clear this obstacle until the prospect has clearly stated that they have a problem, or are actively looking for an improvement. There is no point in pitching a solution if the prospect does not agree that they have a problem.

3. **Solution obstacle:** Once you confirm that there is a problem, there are usually plenty of ways that it can be solved. You need to present your solution as superior to the alternatives.

4. **Meeting obstacle:** Once the prospect realises that your solution can help them, and only then, you can start suggesting a meeting. Why should they work with you, and not with your competitors?

5. **Transfer obstacle:** If someone else will hold the actual meeting, you need to hand the relationship over smoothly to that other person.

6. **Marketing support:** How quickly your prospect will move down the funnel depends on the quality of your nurturing, but also on marketing support. If you have testimonials, case studies or white papers, or if you are positioned as a guru in your field, that will make the transition as smooth as possible.

I will discuss each obstacle in turn and also tell you how to deal with a No at that stage.

Response obstacle

Successful prospect: 'I am curious.'

Receiving a response in some ways means you are over the first hurdle, but also presents your first obstacle. It marks the transition from automated outreach to manual nurture.

If you have gotten this far, you have a general idea who the automation tool sent the messages to. You have targeted your ideal client with well-crafted hooks, and they have started to respond to the campaign.

An essential switch needs to happen here. You are no longer talking to an audience. You are talking to a single person. That particular person is a human being, with their own emotions, fears, struggles and desires. You can't assume that all the people you have targeted have a particular problem or behave in a particular way. When you're addressing an audience you can assume what unites them based on your research, but when talking to an individual, you need to ask. If you don't make this switch here, you will not be able to engage with the individual who has responded to you.

Now that you're talking to an individual, do everything you can to understand them better. As a minimum check out their LinkedIn profile and their company website. Remember, you are building a relationship, so work hard on getting to know them.

'No' at the response obstacle stage

Even if you have the perfect message hooks, there are always people who state clearly that they don't want to have anything to do with you. There is not much you can do about this, since you are at the beginning of the process. They don't know you – but they don't even want to know you.

And that is OK. Some people don't want help, or they don't appreciate external support from a consultant, or from software. It would take you too much effort to convert one No at this stage than at any other stage. So, honestly, it's not worth it. You don't need to curse them out or remove them from your network. Just craft a polite answer, and end things with good manners.

If you are using LinkedIn outreach, keep the person in your connections list. This means that they can still see your posts, and might change their mind. You can also see their posts, giving you access to their thoughts and problems. So a broader nurture strategy with frequent social posting can help here.

If you have approached them over email, and they are not interested in entering a relationship but have not actually opted out of your email list, you can add them to your database (depending on applicable data protection laws) and send a few cold emails once in a while. This way, they can be reminded of you over time, and get in touch when they are ready. Of course, if they opt out, there is not much more you can do.

Problem obstacle

Successful prospect: 'I have a stated problem.'

The problem obstacle is usually the trickiest to over-come and you'll probably lose most of the prospects at this stage.

When someone responds to your campaign, the next stage is to get them to admit that they have a problem. It doesn't always have to be a problem, as such – it might be an expression of a wish to move towards a desired future state. They want or need something.

You can't assume that they have the problem, and you can't ask them directly if they have it. Remember, assumptions work with a broad audience, not with individuals. It can be especially disastrous to make assumptions based on demographics. I am a busy male company owner but that doesn't mean I don't want to cook for my family. Or that my wife, BizzBee's Co-Founder, doesn't get her share of the heavy lifting around the house, like fixing appliances. So instead of making assumptions, you need to ask.

On the other hand, you can't ask a complete stranger a complex, profound question. You really can't. Yet I see people do that every day on LinkedIn or email. Would you answer these questions for a complete stranger?

- What is currently holding you or your business back from success?

- What are your biggest fears?

- Is your company succeeding or struggling?

- What are the main problems you or your business face at the moment?

- What is your current revenue?

I would certainly not. And yet, people ask them – directly.

Rather than ask such challenging direct questions, start building a relationship to the point where the prospect will be more open to answering simpler questions, before moving to more complex ones.

Imagine you are meeting someone in a bar for the first time. You would start with some small talk. The weather is often the most general and neutral topic. Sports is another one, or a current happening. Covid-19 was an excellent icebreaker for a long time. A simple question like 'How was your day?' could provide you with a lot of information.

If you want to really build a relationship, you need to start sharing something about yourself as well. Otherwise it's more like an interview than a conversation.

- You say you have kids; they have kids as well = you have a great topic to chat about

- You like surfing; they don't = you move on to another topic

- They like cats; you don't = you show a polite interest, then move on to another topic.

Once you have exchanged some basic mutual information, you can move towards more targeted questions aimed at understanding whether they have a problem you can solve. 'How are you currently doing [something]?' is usually a great way to move towards business talk. Now, this really depends on the target (CEO, HR manager, financial director) and the solution you offer (leads, HR SaaS, accounting services). But the questions should start off more general, and then get narrower based on the responses you receive. And don't forget, to build a relationship you need to tell them about your business as well.

By this stage, a cold prospect is no longer a cold prospect. They are a friend, a colleague, a fellow business person. And you are no longer a stranger, so you can start talking about their problems with them.

Not all prospects will get to this stage. Not everyone you approach will have a problem or a desire to change something. And that is not to be taken personally. It just means that at the moment, they aren't ready to hear more about your solution.

Only when you confirm their problem can you move to the next stage. You might even get responses from the prospects with a question, such as 'What would you advise?' – which is an opening for the next stage.

'No' at the problem obstacle stage

This means that the prospect fails to acknowledge that they have a problem. This negative answer is far better than the previous one; it's an answer you can work with and try to convert to a Yes.

After a No, you have an opportunity to ask an open-ended question that will push the prospect to explain in more detail – which helps you to better understand their position and obstacles, so you can address them more adequately.

- 'What do you mean?'

- 'Why do you think that?'

- 'Can you elaborate on that?'

- Or a simple 'Why not?'

These kinds of questions are gateways to a more insightful answer. An answer that will help you to ask better questions.

Solution obstacle

Successful prospect: 'This solution will work for me.'

Now we have a stated problem, or a desire to seize an opportunity. Can you make your pitch? Well, not yet. You only have a stated problem. You are still missing some other aspects.

How can you make your type of solution (not your own unique solution, you are still not pitching yet) look superior to the available alternatives? As usual, there are multiple possible solutions to a single problem.

For example, my problem could be that I want more leads to grow my business. There are many ways to get more leads – SEO, content development, social media, paid ads, cold prospecting, organising events, participating in conferences or exhibitions and plenty more. Each of them has advantages and disadvantages. So why and how is your channel, or type of approach, better than the alternatives? How should your cold prospect choose between all these ways of solving the same problem?

If you ask the right questions, you can easily understand which stage the prospect has reached in trying to solve their problem. Here are a few questions for this particular example:

- Great to hear that you are interested in getting more leads. What have you tried so far to generate leads? Are you satisfied with the results?

- (If they said yes:) What kind of results did you achieve?

- (If they said no:) What went wrong? Have you considered other ways of generating leads?

This kind of questioning will tell you what the prospect has tried, or is curious to try. If they haven't tried any lead generation solutions, you can find out which ways of generating leads they might consider. If they tried cold prospecting, you are surely interested in hearing more about that. Are they doing it in-house or outsourcing? Do they think they can do better, and so on?

Just remember, you are not interviewing the prospect; you are building a relationship. Which means you also need to share your experiences, positive or negative. Following the lead generation example, you can go on to say, for example, that you've tried paid Facebook ads, but they didn't work for you, so you are wondering if Facebook ads work for them.

You are creating an opening for the prospect's input, opinions, thoughts.

Your goal for this section is to assure the prospect that your type of solution can work specifically for their business. You can show some reports, statistics or even case studies showing how a solution like yours has helped similar companies to theirs. The goal is to convince them that your type of solution is superior to others.

'No' at the solution obstacle stage

The prospect is aware that they have a problem, but they disagree that your type of solution is the best for them. In other words, they need more convincing.

Again, 'Why?' is an open question that can give you some insights. Perhaps they've tried it before and got terrible results. Maybe they simply don't believe that this type of solution will solve their problem. Or maybe they don't understand or know that your solution works and are afraid to try it. Pay close attention – these answers each require a completely different approach to address them properly.

If they've tried a similar solution before, you need to convince them that one bad experience doesn't mean that they should stop trying. And you should show plenty of good experiences to overcome that one bad experience.

If they don't believe in this type of solution, you need to use a lot of statistics, case studies and examples to persuade them otherwise.

If they don't understand the solution, you need to patiently educate them about it so they can appreciate the value.

But none of this will happen if they say No, and you just leave the conversation without asking 'Why?'

Meeting obstacle

Successful prospect: 'You can help me with my problem. I want to set up a meeting.'

Now you have the prospect engaged. They are aware that they have a problem, and believe that your type of solution can solve it. Now they are actively looking for a solution for their problem.

Now is the time for your pitch. Have in mind that, instead of a sales pitch, you are pitching for a short call or a meeting. But you need to structure the pitch as an answer to their problem. How does your solution solve their problem? How is your solution better than all your competitors'? It's likely that there are both cheaper and more expensive options, and competitors who provide more or fewer features and more or less value. What makes you stand out from the crowd?

191

One major advantage is that you have already established a relationship. You know one another, so your prospect is more likely to choose your solution. Knowing your unique selling point (USP) can also help here, as you can pitch your uniqueness – something that your competitors don't have.

Marketing assets like testimonials, references and case studies come in handy. If you have examples of working with companies similar to your prospect, that works like magic. If you come to me, and show me how you've solved my problem in companies that are similar to mine (even competitors), then I'll rest assured you can also help me.

Now they've reached the bottom of the funnel. You are friends with them. You know their problem. You have assured them that your type of solution will work for them and that your unique solution is the best.

Now you can introduce the meeting element. You can also add some **scarcity** or **urgency** elements.

An excellent example of scarcity is that although you want to help, you have limited capacity in your schedule. This makes them want to be fitted in.

A good example of urgency is that you are planning on starting a group of students in the next three days, or there is a discount that ends in the next forty-eight hours. These tactics will usually increase their desire to cross the meeting obstacle and want to schedule a call with you faster.

Now that a prospect wants a meeting, it is only an administrative step to set up the meeting.

'No' at the meeting obstacle stage

So they've agreed that your type of solution is the most appropriate, but are still not interested in talking to you specifically. You probably didn't establish enough credibility for yourself or your business. Or they still don't trust you to handle their problem. A simple 'Why not?' will give you insight into what is going on in their head – what concerns or fears they have that are preventing them from moving forward.

Another way is to present the meeting as a free value offer. Instead of offering a sales meeting, you can position it as a free consultation or a free audit of their existing systems. This way, they might reconsider because it sounds like something they will benefit from.

Transfer obstacle (optional)

Successful prospect: 'I am happy to do the meeting with someone else.'

If you are holding the meetings, you can simply skip this step. However, if you are an agency or working as BDR/SDR and someone else needs to do the actual meeting, then there is another obstacle that you need to overcome. It is the transfer obstacle – you could bring a prospect to this stage, and then lose them when you mention that you will transfer them to another person. They built the relationship with you, and might decline the meeting once you tell them that it is with someone else.

You have a prospect interested in scheduling a meeting. How can you transfer the meeting to the client (for agencies) or to a senior sales representative (for SDR/BDR)? You need to introduce the new person as superior to you.

You can do this in various ways.

The examples below are just ideas on how you can make the transition smooth, and conversational rather than a request for approval.

- 'I just had a chat with my colleague about your problem, and they had a few fantastic ideas about how we can help you. Perhaps it is better to connect you with them so that they can present them to you? They are the best in our company.'

- 'I just talked with my CEO about you, and I got them excited about your business. This is a rare case, but they wanted to get on the call with you, because they have two ideas that can help your business.'

'No' at the transfer obstacle stage

They want a meeting, but don't want to have a meeting with the new person you are trying to introduce. This can happen if you established such a good relationship with them that they don't want to move away from you. Or you didn't present the new person as superior to you and make clear that it's in the prospect's best interest to talk to them, rather than you.

The simplest way is for you to be present on the call and to introduce the new person. You can connect with the prospect, and then introduce your colleague or client as someone with more experience, or someone who has worked with similar companies and can better address their needs. That always works; if you tell me that there is someone with more expertise in your team, and I trust you, I would definitely want help from the best person possible.

It's harder if you won't be on the call. Then you need to convince the prospect that it is in their best interest to take the call with your colleague rather than you. But the transition must be perfect – otherwise you lose a prospect that you've worked hard to bring to this stage.

Marketing support

Nurturing prospects can be hard – trying to approach a cold prospect, and convince them that your product can actually help them. Remember how you would feel if a complete stranger approached you and offered you a pill that would solve some of your problems. 'I've never met this person, I've never heard about the brand and they're asking me to pay a significant amount of money? Feels kind of shady to me.'

This is where the marketing support comes in. The scenario is the same, but you know the brand of the pill and you've heard a lot of people talking about it and it worked miracles for your friends. So, would you be more likely to try it? Probably.

When we started, I really underestimated the importance of strong marketing materials. It took us a few years to understand that clients who have these get far better results than those who don't. Now we employ copywriters, so we can also help clients with their marketing.

Marketing is just a booster for your nurturing efforts. You could still do successful nurturing without the marketing help, but it would be much harder.

Marketing can't work miracles, but if a prospect is considering your offer, it can achieve the extra push you need to get a positive response at each stage. However, you need different marketing support for the different stages.

In this section, we will look at how marketing can support outreach and make it easier, and go over several marketing strategies that could significantly improve your outreach campaign. The more of the marketing assets mentioned in this section you have, the better. Some of them will overlap and there is no overall marketing plan outline – that will be unique for each prospect.

First impression: LinkedIn or website

During cold outreach, you are approaching complete strangers. And believe me, they won't spend hours, or even minutes, checking you out to understand your background. You have a small window of a few seconds to make a good first impression.

Of course, if you get through that first moment, you will have plenty of opportunities to prove your value and expertise – but if you fail, it is hard to go back.

When you approach someone on **LinkedIn**, your first impression is your LinkedIn profile. When anyone sends me a connection request, I look at the invitation message but I also have a quick glance at their profile – the image, the title, the description. I spend less than thirty seconds deciding whether I want to accept their connection. So as we discussed in the previous chapter, without an engaging LinkedIn profile, you will miss a lot of opportunities.

When approaching via email, the first impression, beyond the content of the messages you send, is your **website**. If I am considering whether to respond to a cold email, I will have a quick look at the sender's website, just to see if I understand what it is about. So if your website is outdated, or it fails to communicate what you do, you will lose a lot of prospects.

These are the basics. Would you like to be perceived as a professional or an amateur? Well, your LinkedIn profile and your website are the main factors in this. Look at them again to make sure they support your current campaign. Does your website communicate your value proposition well? Does your profile make people feel that they want to be part of your network?

Blog posts

Blog posts are the most common assets to share during the outreach sequence, or after someone shows some interest. Your marketing team can create articles that are highly targeted and specific. This will give some value to the cold prospect, which can, in turn, make them consider responding to your campaign. Here are some examples.

- 'How can [your ideal target] get [their desire] without [obstacle]?' – eg How can high-ticket service providers get new leads without paid ads?

- 'The X best ways to get [results] without [obstacle]' – eg The three best ways to get leads without spending a fortune.

These blogs can be shared via email (as news), directly as a LinkedIn message (as a relevant article you think will help your prospect) or as a post on your social media. In any case, having several posts that are highly valuable to your targets can significantly improve the response rate.

When writing a blog post, keep one thing in mind. Which obstacle are you trying to overcome? You should only tackle one obstacle per article. If you are trying to convince readers that they have a problem, don't push them towards your solution – that feels biased. If I read an article stating a problem that I have, and it ends by trying to sell me the author's solution it loses credibility.

A few weeks ago I went shopping for jeans. I went into a well-stocked jeans shop, but because I am plus size, my options are quite limited. So instead of asking for a particular cut, my first question is about size availability. Then I decide between the designs that come in my size. No point in deciding I like particular jeans only to realise that they don't have my size in that design.

Anyway, I liked one pair, so I tried them on. They looked awful on me. My wife agreed, and she has far better taste than me. But the saleswoman was so flattering. She made a lot of comments on how well the jeans fitted me. If I was having doubts, she might have convinced me. But I was absolutely sure she was lying. Then it hit me. She didn't care whether the jeans looked good on me. She cared about making a sale and getting a commission. Her advice was not in my best interest. How can you get honest advice for a problem from someone who is trying to sell you the solution?

The same is true in every kind of business. Imagine someone approaches you and tells you that Facebook ads give the best results, and then pitches you their Facebook ad service. Is the person really trying to help you, or do they have their own interest at heart? I call that biased truth. It's similar when it comes to blogs. So, do one thing at a time in your posts. Stick to a single obstacle, don't use the same post to try to explain a problem, evaluate alternatives and show your superior solution. It just doesn't work. If you try to explain a problem – focus solely on the problem. If you want to evaluate alternatives – keep your focus on the comparison.

Email newsletter

With a weekly or monthly newsletter, you remind the prospect that you exist. If you have a strong newsletter (with a lot of content that adds value), you position yourself as the go-to person on the subject. If they need something, you are then the first person they will call. And that can be a few weeks or a few months later.

I've seen a lot of newsletters where the main focus is on the company that's issuing the newsletter. A series of promotions like 'why you should hire us', 'why we are the best' and similar content isn't really a newsletter – it is more like a sales leaflet. And of course, prospects respond by ignoring it or unsubscribing.

Your newsletter should be about the prospects. And only about them. Your goal is not to sell them anything, but to make them curious, engaged and moving towards a point where they might show interest in the type of solution you are offering. A typical newsletter should have several sections, and each section should either provide value or be entertaining. When we built our first newsletter, we had the following structure:

- **Header:** An image that captures the attention of the reader.

- **Introduction:** Tell the prospects about the newsletter's theme or topic, so they can decide whether they should read it.

- **Main value:** We promoted our weekly blog on the subject, with some bullet points on why they should read it.

- **Fun section:** A meme or a funny image.

- **Curated content:** So that it wasn't all about BizzBee, we included the latest trends, blogs and news on the topic.

- **Recommendation by our employee:** Depending on the theme, one of our team recommends a tool, a book, a course etc that could help the reader do something better, faster or more efficiently.

- **Curated wisdom:** A quote that one of our team is driven by. It gives a perspective on what we believe in and what we stand for.

You'll notice that we don't try to sell anything. Our goal is to maintain credibility and expertise, and showcase our personality by sharing our own posts and curated content.

The purpose of the newsletter is not to get new clients, but to nurture the relationship with your existing prospects, so they will get in touch with you when they are ready, or when they need you.

Thought leadership

Showing evidence of thought leadership through your social posts and on email builds your credibility. Its primary marketing purpose is to soften prospects to connect with you, want to engage with you and want to work with you.

Through your relationship with the prospect, they can be constantly exposed to your posts on LinkedIn, Facebook, Twitter, Instagram, etc. And many new platforms will undoubtedly arise.

You can use any of these platforms, or email, to share some of the blogs you've created, but thought leadership goes deeper than that. A thought leader does not share only about their own business. They are interested in several subjects (usually their top five) and all the topics they share are around these key themes. When I was building my thought leadership plan, I chose four categories to share:

- **Business posts:** Obviously, I need to share business thoughts, posts, topics and curated posts to help build my credibility as an expert in the field. Some of the posts can be mine. Some can be curated from other platforms or sources.

- **Family posts:** I know it might feel weird to share posts about your wife, kids and parents, but try it. First, you will show that you are not all about business. Second, people will connect with you on an entirely new level. When I shared a photo playing with my son, and crafted some intriguing copy, the engagement was fantastic. Other parents in particular felt they were able to connect with me.

- **Travel posts:** I love to explore new places whenever I can. Why would I hide this from my followers (or new prospects who have just agreed to connect with me)? I want to paint a picture of a person, not a robot whose life revolves solely around work. If you share your personal passion, people will feel more connected to you.

- **Personal development posts:** If you really want to connect to your audience, you need to open up to them. As I learn new things, I share them with my community. When I decided to write a book, I posted about it and got loads of engagement.

What happens when you start posting on these four categories? In short, miracles. Sharing your stories and your journey makes people feel that they can connect with you and trust you, and shows them that you are not a scammer or a fake. Plus, as you get comfortable with sharing aspects of yourself, there are personal benefits for you.

Simple assets/e-books

I have published seven e-books and three digital assets, so I can tell you how they can work for you. You show your prospects that you understand them and that you've made an effort to summarise your key findings into an e-book or a PDF file for their benefit.

Digital assets are an easier route. First, you need to understand what your ideal target needs, and then create some kind of marketing content for it. This can be an extended blog post or PDF briefing on (to give examples from my own business) the top ten tools you can use for lead generation, or twelve Excel formulas for lead generation, and so on.

You are not expected to deliver miracles, or fifty-plus pages of content. You just need to sum up a few insights or tips and tricks that you've figured out and want to share with the world. If people find your content relevant, they will subscribe to get more.

Crafting an **e-book** (a mini-book of 5,000–10,000 words on how you solve a particular problem) is more work – it requires experience and the ability to think through and describe a process. However, producing highly targeted e-books could really help your prospecting.

I've seen companies outsource the e-book writing process, and fail big time. You can't really expect someone with only basic knowledge in your industry, or an external person, to provide the in-depth insight that is required. So my advice is to create your e-book in-house.

Be clear about what your goal for the e-book is. If you are trying to educate people on your subject, then it should provide the response to a problem or obstacle. Usually, e-books are in the 'how-to' area. If you provide expert insights, based on your experience, or cover a niche target, then the e-book can be a credibility booster.

Social proof

You will get to a stage when the prospect asks – why you? This is your opportunity to pitch, to show how your solution has already helped plenty of businesses. For a mature company, this is a great opportunity to show its track record.

The simplest form of social proof is a **testimonial**. If a company is happy with your services, ask for a testimonial. Ideally this will say that you have collaborated and they are thrilled with the process or the outcome.

If the marketing department manages to get testimonials from businesses similar to your ideal client, things get easier. If a supplier tells me that they have done the same work with a company similar to mine, or my competitors, then I know that they have industry-specific experience and that they can help me.

It is up to the marketing team to generate testimonials that will support the outreach process, and increase the response rate. You may not have testimonials if you are new, but your response rate will significantly improve if you can get them.

A **case study** is a deeper level of testimonial. It tells the whole story of how a company similar to the prospect's reached out to your business, how you identified their problems and helped them get the results they wanted.

If a cold prospect sees one, two or three case studies of similar businesses and the type of results you've managed to achieve, that will definitely help the conversion process.

One-time offer

Throughout the nurturing process, you might get to a point where you have connected with the prospect, and you are on the right track. At this stage, you need to move them towards a meeting. But how?

Common ways to do this are either to show them they need the meeting or introduce a promotion that we call an OTO – one-time offer.

The purpose of the OTO is to advance all prospects who are considering whether to move forward – to push them towards a meeting. For this purpose, we need to create several offers with a limited expiration date and limited availability. As mentioned above, **scarcity** and **urgency** are the best driving forces for people to take action.

Chapter takeaway

A cold lead has responded to your outreach sequence. It's still not time to celebrate. This is where you need to move the conversation from one-to-many to one-to-one.

From this point you need to see the conversation as a set of obstacles that you need to overcome in order to get to the meeting. By getting a response, you have passed the **response obstacle**.

Some respondents will have clear need of your services and jump on a call. An easy win. Others will show that they are not interested in your service. Your response will vary depending on which stage they lose interest at.

The majority of your respondents are at an in-between stage. They will engage in conversation but at some point will need additional effort. If you have passed the response obstacle, you know that the cold prospect is curious.

The second hurdle is the **problem obstacle**. You want to get this prospect to admit they have a problem, or acknowledge interest in the opportunity at hand. You can't move them down the funnel until they make that statement in some form, and you will need to build the relationship for this to happen. Asking follow-up and open questions can give you great insight into their needs. You will know that you have cleared the problem obstacle when they acknowledge the problem or the opportunity.

The third is the **solution obstacle**. The goal here is to show them that your type of solution is the best for them, compared with alternatives (not competitors, but alternatives). You will know you have cleared this obstacle when they acknowledge that your type of solution will work for them.

The fourth obstacle is the **meeting obstacle**. They now believe that your type of solution will work. Why should they get it from you, and not your competitors? Showing your USP will differentiate you. You will know you have succeeded when you convince them that you are the right partner for them, and they want to schedule a meeting.

For agencies and BDR/SDRs there is another obstacle, which is the **transfer obstacle**: transferring the lead to the senior sales representative. You need a clear value proposition for the warm lead to be comfortable about meeting someone else.

HONEY TASTING FRAMEWORK
FOR LEAD NURTURING

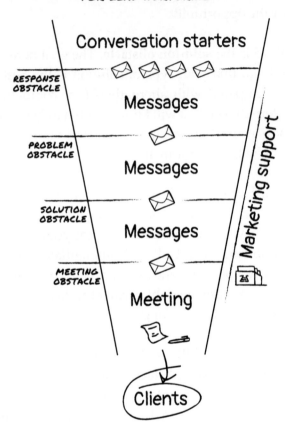

6
Campaign Optimisation (Flavour Refining)

The optimisation framework

Did you know that bees have such a tendency for optimisation that they've even contributed to science? I want to introduce you to the Bees Algorithm,[12] a population-based search algorithm developed in 2005.

What does it have to do with bees?

It was inspired by the natural foraging behaviour of honey bees to find the optimal solution. A colony of honey bees can extend itself over long distances (even more than 10 km) and in multiple directions

---

12 DT Pham et al, *Bee Algorithm – A Novel Approach to Function Optimisation* (Manufacturing Engineering Centre, Cardiff University, 2005)

simultaneously to harvest nectar from multiple food sources. The colony employs only one-quarter of its members as scout or forager bees. The scouts forage for promising flower patches. They don't stop when they have found a flower patch – they keep looking, in the hope of finding an even better one.

When the scout bees return to the hive, they inform their peers of the food source's quality. The scout bees deposit their nectar and hit the dance floor in front of the hive. Yes, you read that right. They communicate with the other bees by performing their 'waggle dance'.

The waggle dance is named after the waggling run (in which the dancing bees produce a loud buzzing sound by moving their bodies from side to side), which the scout bees use to communicate information about the food source to the rest of the colony. Through the dance, the scout bees tell the rest of the hive about the quality of the nectar, how far it is from the hive and in which direction. Pretty impressive.

This is not the only algorithm inspired by bees. The key is that bees make a point of communicating to do a better job. We can use this as a reminder to always optimise our outreach processes and never lose hope of finding a better source of nectar.

The first thing you need to help you improve is a good record of what your outreach has achieved. This can feel like a load of extra admin, to go over everything you've just done and record it. And in most cases it is. But it can be much more. A good record can give you insight about where to focus your outreach. It can also help you understand which messages resonate with your target audience, and which simply do not.

Without a good campaign report, optimisation is impossible. You can't improve the campaign if you don't know how it is performing, so at this stage in the ZZ Framework, focus on monitoring your metrics.

We created a LinkedIn campaign for a mindset coaching business from Ireland, targeting self-employed business owners in Ireland. We did everything right – great profile, great messages and fantastic target. But it did not work. We only had a 7% acceptance rate, which was not enough on which to base a campaign. Once our 7% accepted, the other metrics were pretty good, so we knew that the acceptance rate was the problem – the target audience was not connecting, so we were doing something wrong.

We made a small tweak on the client's LinkedIn profile, just changing the headline. A tiny tweak when you look at the big picture of the outreach overall. But after that change, the acceptance rate rose to 30% – an increase of 23% and a valuable lesson learned. Without a clear report we would not have known what adjustment to make.

Before diving into reporting, let's establish some common-sense ground rules. If it was up to me, I would record absolutely everything. From time spent on each activity to the funnel response rate on different channels. In addition, I would closely follow the impact of each message and its conversion rate. I would also record twenty to fifty additional things that most people would not bother with.

In the past I've fallen into the trap of reporting just for the sake of reporting, to the point where my team spent almost half their time reporting on their activities. I felt justified in my commitment to data-gathering. If I had a report on everything, I could be clear about what worked and what didn't and create any report I might need at any stage in the future. And that was magic for me. But maintaining that level of reporting was just exhausting. Perhaps it helped me at the beginning of the outreach process, when I really needed to measure everything. But we are busy, and need a few key pieces to help us today, rather than a complete palette of data to be interpreted later. Remember that the sole purpose of reporting at this point is to provide insight on your campaign's progress.

Now, instead of wasting time on tracking everything, we've evolved. I would rather know about five to ten key aspects, than have data on 100 aspects and lose a lot of time in interpretation. We still need reporting.

One purpose is to measure the benefits we've created for our clients. But what is more important is to test and understand what works when we offer specific services to particular targets. If we can understand this, then we have a winning solution.

I wish I could test all my ideas on my clients, but I don't think that a client would willingly agree to be a lab rat. So, BizzBee created five accounts (each with a LinkedIn profile and an email) purely for experimentation and testing. At first we just wanted to test different aspects of our outreach. When I understood the importance of these tests, we developed BizzBee Laboratory. This is a dedicated resource with the primary goal of providing insight into how outreach works and the variables that affect campaign results. We are able to use that insight to help our clients get better results. That is the ultimate goal.

When measuring outreach, we need to set up metrics both for email and for LinkedIn, the two outreach strategies covered in this book. These two channels have a few differences in approach at the beginning, as we have seen, but they both work towards the same goal – scheduling a meeting.

Inspired by the bee story, we named the campaign optimisation framework the Flavour Refining Framework.

FLAVOUR REFINING FRAMEWORK
FOR CAMPAIGN OPTIMISATION

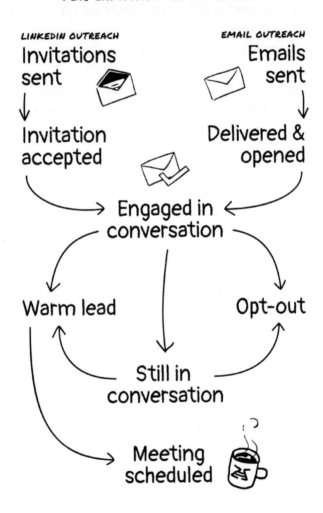

This chapter is dedicated to issues specific to LinkedIn and to email, and then looks at those relevant for both. For LinkedIn, we will look at:

- **LinkedIn invitations sent:** Establishing a predictable number of invitations that are sent daily / weekly / monthly. This is the starting measure for any LinkedIn campaign – how many new people are you adding to your funnel?

- **Invitations accepted:** Looking at the cold prospects who accept the invitation message and will then be included in the outreach sequence. You can't send any follow-up until your invitation is accepted.

For email sequence:

- **Emails sent:** The number of emails being sent in the outreach campaign.

- **Emails delivered and opened:** How many are being received and opened by the recipient?

Then we look at cross-campaign conversion rates.

- **Response rate:** How many people engaged with the campaign. This can be measured separately for LinkedIn and email, and is the starting point for nurture based on the type of response.

- Negative responses: The number of people who say they are not interested or unsubscribe from the email list.

- Positive responses: The number of people who were excited and wanted to hear more from you.

- Neutral responses: The number of people who were neither positive nor negative, but continued with the conversation. These need to be nurtured towards positive responses. And of course, some of them will unsubscribe as well.

• **Meetings:** The number of people who schedule a meeting with you, as well as the quality of meetings scheduled.

LinkedIn invitation and acceptance rate

Executing a LinkedIn campaign without any metrics is a shot in the dark so let's change that. These are the metrics you should have in mind.

Invitations sent

Optimisation question: Do you consistently reach out to new prospects daily? How do you avoid delays?

You must send new invitations on a daily, weekly and monthly basis. It is the only way to have a stable stream of new leads every week.

Our target is to send 70–100 invitations per week. You can send them manually or automatically, but the key point here is consistency. You do the maths. Sending 100 invitations per week is 400 invitations per month, which is 48,000 invitations per year. That is the capacity of a single LinkedIn profile. And you can use several profiles.

There was a time when we were able to send 100+ invitations per day, but people started spamming the platform, making it hard to genuinely reach people. Linkedin introduced restrictions just to ensure that quality relationships are nurtured.

The invitation sent is a metric that will tell you whether your funnel is slowing down, or whether you or your team are forgetting the key entry step. I check this as a key performance indicator (KPI) every week. Have we sent around 100 new invitations? If not, why? What happened?

Bear in mind that LinkedIn limits the maximum number of pending invitations. This means that you should remove old pending invitations at least once a month, to make space for new ones. Not everyone on LinkedIn checks their profile every day, and they are not waiting for your invitation.

Invitations accepted

Optimisation question: How can you improve your LinkedIn acceptance rate?

The number of invitations to connect accepted is the first big metric that you can actually start analysing. How many people accept you on a weekly or monthly basis?

As this is the starting point of the LinkedIn funnel, the more people who accept, the more will be exposed to the messages you've crafted in the previous chapters. It is a pity to spend a lot of effort on the planning stage, and then get few prospects to whom you can actually send your message sequence.

Our benchmark for the acceptance rate is in the range of 30–50%. This means that one out of three or one out of two invitations results in a prospect becoming part of your network. I have managed to get a 75% acceptance rate for some clients, and others have only had 20% acceptance. But a benchmark shows you how you rank compared with other campaigns. Don't treat this number too seriously, because it varies quite a lot, depending on the target, solution, profile, etc. You need to make your own benchmark.

There are variables that can be adjusted to improve the acceptance rate. Whenever we get worse results than the average, we look at three variables that we can affect and control:

1. **The invitation message:** If you have a low acceptance rate, the invitation message is the first thing you need to revisit. Does it seem spammy?

We always aim for less intrusive, short, fairly generic invitation messages, because we want to get accepted. Once we get accepted, we can send more messages and build a relationship. But if they don't accept us, we don't have a second chance.

2. **The LinkedIn profile:** Is the profile communicating the right message to your target audience?

   Remember that an average person who receives your invitation will spend five to ten seconds in total deciding whether to accept you. In that small window, if your profile seems salesy, or spammy, or off, that is it. It has to be not only perfect, but perfect for your target audience.

   I had a client who had a strong profile – he was an investor, founder of several start-ups, adviser. He had an MBA from Harvard. His photo and background were impeccable. He was targeting doctors for his AI technology in medicine. And although he had a strong profile, it did not resonate with his target audience.

   Once we tweaked his profile to make it clear that his AI solution was helping doctors make the right diagnosis, the acceptance rate soared.

3. **The target audience:** Even if you have the perfect profile and the perfect invitation message, these are worthless if you are not talking to the right target. If your acceptance rate is quite

low, perhaps you need to look at a different target audience? Or perhaps you should narrow the target filter – by focusing on second-tier connections and people active in the past thirty days.

However, there are a few variables that you can't control, and that you should take into consideration when analysing the acceptance rate.

We always experience a drop in acceptance rates during summer. Many countries take a long summer break (Nordic countries take July and August off) and you really cannot expect anyone to respond on their holiday.

Religious holidays also affect the rate. There are two Christmases. For the majority of the world, Catholic Christmas means that December is more or less a holiday. On the other hand, Orthodox Christmas (which is celebrated by Belarus, Egypt, Ethiopia, Georgia, Kazakhstan, Macedonia, Moldova, Montenegro, Serbia, Russia and Ukraine) means that January is a holiday month in these countries. In Muslim countries and communities, people are not very responsive to outreach in Ramadan (which lasts a month and shifts every year).

EXTRA HONEY: LINKEDIN CAMPAIGN REPORT

To help you stay aware of all the factors that can affect your campaign, we have created a LinkedIn campaign report template. You'll find it on our book resource page: www.BizzBeeSolutions.com/book-resources.

This is the report sheet for our own LinkedIn campaigns and those of our clients. We improve it constantly. We share this with you to not only help you define and measure your LinkedIn outbound KPIs, but so you can have a clear view of the direction you are heading in. This way you can keep on experimenting with your LinkedIn outreach, measure the outcomes and improve them.

Email sending, delivery and open rate

Optimisation question: How can you maximise your email open rate?

Similar to LinkedIn, we also need insight from our email delivery metrics so that we can adjust the email campaign to get better results.

Emails sent, your first metric, can be different from the number of emails you've uploaded to the automation. You might have some invalid emails, which have been excluded. As long as the mismatch is a small number, you are OK.

Messages delivered should be almost identical to **messages sent** if you made a good job of your database. There could be a small variation if some of the emails bounced, or were rejected by the recipient's email provider.

However, if you hadn't properly warmed up the domain or email you created, your email provider might block the majority of your messages.

Once your emails have reached the recipient, you need to analyse the **open rate**. There are a few variables that can affect this. Has your email ended up in the recipient's spam folder? In this case, you should again work on improving your email deliverability. The second one is the subject line. If the subject line does not catch the attention of the cold prospect, they can delete the message without even opening it. Try changing the subject line to improve the open rate. You can try several subjects and see what works best.

The third variable in the open rate is the delivery time. There are a lot of reports on the best time to send an email. If everyone follows the same recommendations, then your email won't get far. It's best to test for yourself and find the time that gives you the best open rate.

EXTRA HONEY: EMAIL MARKETING REPORT
You can find our email marketing report on our book resource page: www.BizzBeeSolutions.com/book-resources.

224

Response rate

Optimisation question: How can you improve your response rate?

In a LinkedIn campaign, once your cold prospect accepts you in their network, you move the prospect to your predefined sequence of messages.

For email, once you improve the delivery and open rate, the next step is to start measuring responses. Of course you are interested in how many people are responding to the message sequence and how to improve the response rate. But an even more important question is: 'What was their response?'

You can affect the response rate by improving the outreach process, but also by improving your overall marketing and credibility. Outreach is not an independent activity; it is aligned with your other marketing activities. For example, a good or bad website will significantly affect the response rate, as will the attractiveness of the solution you offer. So, improving your other marketing efforts can also boost your response rate.

Looking at the outreach process itself, there are tweaks you can make to boost the response rate. The most obvious is the **message sequence**. If people read your three to five messages and decide to ignore you, you need to improve your messages, so they can resonate better with your target audience.

Second, it could be that your **target** does not have the problem you are trying to solve, so although your messages are fantastic you will not get a response. In this case you need to re-evaluate the target.

Third (and this is not something you can do anything about) it could mean that the target you are pitching to is **not very active online**. Ideally, you would have thought about this at the planning stage, while defining your ICP.

Some industries simply do not have a digital focus. We've tried to help clients target doctors, yoga instructors and restaurant chefs. Although we got some responses, the rate was far below our average because these people do most of their work offline.

There are a lot of people on LinkedIn who check their profile once in a while, or perhaps never. They might accept your invitation but not see your follow-up messages.

Type of response

Optimisation question: How do you minimise opt-outs and maximise positive responses? What can you learn from the responses?

Even if you get a response, that does not mean you have a meeting. It only means that the prospect has engaged with your messages, and the next step is to manually nurture them through your funnel.

One of the big advantages of the outreach process is direct market feedback from your target. Even if you get a lot of negative feedback, you can consider that feedback and adjust the offering or marketing effort accordingly.

A **positive** response means that they are interested and want to hear more about your solution. We have had examples of clients responding to our campaigns right away, saying that this is exactly what they needed and they want a meeting, but this happens rarely. If you do get an immediate positive response, get them on a call ASAP. In most cases there will be a conversation before they express their interest.

A **negative** response means that they are not interested in your solution, or they don't even give you the chance to tell them about it. It is worth giving it another try, but if you keep being ignored move on.

The whole point of a funnel is to start with a lot of prospects, and reduce them to the one person who you can actually help and who is interested in your solution. In many cases, people who are not interested will simply unsubscribe from your mailing list. A big unsubscription rate shows that your target and messages don't fit: one of them needs to be changed.

A **neutral** response is a great starting point. It means that they are not excited about your solution, but they are not explicitly telling you to stop bothering them. They are somewhere in between, and you have a small opportunity window when neutral replies might be moved to interested, with only a few that will end up as negative responses.

Knowing the percentage of positive, negative and neutral responses will give you insight into the message sequence, as well as the nurture quality. You will know your nurturing is not working if many of the people move from Maybe to No.

Meetings

Optimisation question: How can you get more meetings out of the nurture process?

What extra qualifications can you add during the nurture process to improve the quality of the meetings? The last metric is the most important. All your effort has been to move cold prospects down the funnel towards a meeting, so it's important to know how many you have managed to get there.

Beyond the quantity, you must know the quality of the meetings. Were the meetings relevant? Or were they a waste of time? This feedback needs to be brought back throughout the funnel to update the target, the messages or the nurture process.

You can gain other insights by analysing the people who reached the meeting stage. What positions do they hold? What industry are they in? Can you tweak the campaign to attract more of these people?

Chapter takeaway

Once the campaign is up and running, you need to start optimising it. And you can't do campaign optimisation without proper reporting in place.

Once the reporting is established, with simple A/B testing you can measure two variables and the feedback from both, and understand what yields a better result. You can do A/B testing on the target, profile, messages, nurture, etc.

By looking at the number of **LinkedIn invitations**, you ensure that you have consistency in the outreach process, as well as a consistent inflow of new leads.

By looking at the **LinkedIn acceptance rate**, you look at potential improvements to the target, message and the profile – because improving the acceptance rate improves the overall success of the outreach campaign.

For email outreach, start looking at email **sending** and **delivery**. This will tell you if you need improvement in the quality of the database as well as the deliverability of the email domain.

The **open rate** will tell you if your emails are ending up in the spam folder, and if you need to work on improving the subject line.

The **response rate** will tell you if you need to change the message sequence or target. However, the **quality of responses** is also a key aspect.

Having more positive responses, and fewer negative responses, is the main focus. Also, to nurture the neutral towards positive responses.

The **meetings** are the last metrics in the outreach sequence. You can work on how to get more meetings from the campaign and how to adjust your nurture process to get better quality meetings.

FLAVOUR REFINING FRAMEWORK
FOR CAMPAIGN OPTIMISATION

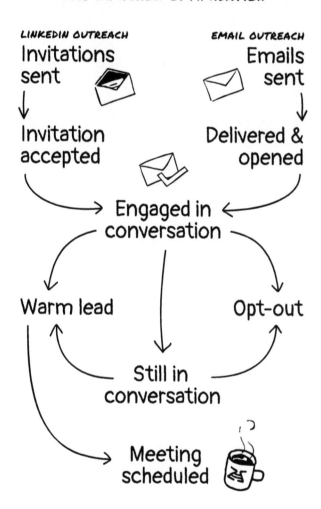

LINKEDIN OUTREACH
Invitations sent

EMAIL OUTREACH
Emails sent

Invitation accepted

Delivered & opened

Engaged in conversation

Warm lead

Opt-out

Still in conversation

Meeting scheduled

Conclusion

You did it – you reached the end of this book, and if you followed the ZZ Framework, you will have lots of likely prospects interested in having a call with you.

As a consultant, I know how it feels selling a premium service. But if your value proposition is right, people will buy. It also feels exhausting to endlessly demonstrate how companies can benefit from your solution. But once they do get the message, they will retain it.

I truly hope that you will find the ZZ Framework approach useful and profitable. I have made quite a lot of clients rich, and I want to share my insights and knowledge so that others can utilise the outreach process.

This takes me back to the time when my wife and I were about to head home from our blissful digital nomad honeymoon to start our own business. I'd worked out that I could get a company up and running for a couple of thousand euros. But the night before we set off home I lay awake, like every business owner does at some point and you probably have, with doom-laden scenarios in my head. What if everything went wrong? Should I take this ultimate risk? Would it be worth it? What about our future family?

But then I figured it out. I can't know how something will end if I haven't started yet. As the hours went by and I lay awake, I remembered those bees, buzzing happily on the flowers they chose, which they knew would be full of the best nectar. And the decision was made. I would go all-in for three months.

Five years later, I'm still here and I'm still inspired by the bees, ready to face all my fears and insecurities and inspire you to do the same.

Let me tell you this. Procrastination never helps. I believe that our fears only ignite it. Growth can only happen when we step out of our comfort zone. Success rarely happens overnight. So the sooner we start, the sooner we can grasp the success. It took me five years to get here. If you start right now, can you imagine what your company will look like in five years?

I like to envision these things. That way, they feel more tangible. I'm confident that the ZZ Framework, Bizz-Bee and I will help at least 500 more companies grow and reach their ideal clients and their true potential. And I definitely see something that might look like another book on the horizon.

So, until then, I wish you successful outreach.

In the meantime, keep in mind that we are always growing our outreach process, and like the bees, we always share what we learn. Check out our latest updates and resources on our website: www.Bizz-BeeSolutions.com.

Acknowledgements

If I had known that writing a book would be such an uphill battle, I probably wouldn't have even started. Luckily, as so often in business, I didn't know beforehand what the obstacles would be. I was in the dark back then. And I had tremendous support to keep me going when things got rough, and I was having doubts, for which I am so grateful.

First of all, hat off to my amazing wife, Maja. Seriously. Thanks for putting up with me – for all the late nights and missed dinners – and all your support. I solemnly swear that from now on, I'll spend less time in front of the computer. I am sure you are even more ecstatic than me for this book to see the light of day.

Special thanks to my son, Metodija, for lifting me up all the times when writing put me down. Your radiant spirit and vigour always bring out the best in me. It was becoming a father that made me decide what I wanted out of life, and showed me the way in my business.

I wouldn't be here without the continuous support from my parents. I'm eternally grateful to my father Metodija and my mother Temjana, for making me understand the importance of education. Not all parents would encourage their child's weird and bold business endeavours. You've stimulated the entrepreneur in me since I was a kid. Respect.

Enormous thanks to my brother, Trajche. You've always been my mentor, my rock and my financial support (whenever needed☺). Without your guidance, neither BizzBee nor the book would have happened.

A big thanks to my extended bee family. As the bees are the most crucial part of the ecosystem, BizzBee's bees are essential to creating this book. Massive thanks to Natasha, Nikolina, Hristina, Stefan and all the other busy bees, current and past. You are the building blocks that contributed to the knowledge and frameworks that exist in this book. Special thanks to Vera, who was involved in the book creation since its inception, and made sure that the book has its own personality.

While I'm on the note of making this book a reality, I would like to thank all BizzBee's clients. My gratitude goes to all our past clients who co-contributed in the creation of our ZZ Framework. You were the basis for our constant improvement. But I'd also like to thank all our current and future clients for putting their trust in us. We're ecstatic to show the world what kind of results our digital outreach frameworks can achieve.

I wouldn't be as proud as I am of this book if it weren't for all my appreciated beta readers. Gordana, Vlatko, Risto, Borjan, Blagoj, Marjan, Mike, Dejan, Reema and Aaron – thank you for taking the time and making the effort not only to read my manuscript, but to send detailed comments and feedback.

Last but not least, huge thanks to Rethink Press and their team for putting their trust in my vision and making this book available to the general public.

The Author

 Dancho Dimkov, MSc Executive MBA CMgr CMC is a B2B outreach consultant, serial entrepreneur and dedicated growth enthusiast. He is on a mission to help SMEs grow while taking into consideration their limited budgets.

His entrepreneurial spirit shone in early childhood, and at just 22 years old he was recognised as a 'Global Innovator for 2009'. This award brought him speaking engagements at major events in different corners of the world, from Finland and India to Brazil and beyond.

He started his career owning a marketing agency, then grew to manage a software company, and he is now the proud owner of the management consultancy BizzBee Solutions. This career journey gave him the experience and tools to make the lives of those particular service providers easier. As the founder and CEO of BizzBee Solutions, he has helped over 400 companies, leading to the '40 under 40 award'.

Dancho always has a bee in his bonnet about selling and outreach, hence the podcasts and interviews. He enjoys both the role as a host and as a guest. He currently lives in Skopje with his loving wife and adorable son, and keeps working to eradicate digital outreach fever, one client at a time.

Connect with him at:

⊕ DanchoDimkov.com

in linkedin.com/in/DancoDimkov

f facebook.com/Dancho.Dimkov.98

If you want to embark on the outreach journey yourself but need some help, make sure you contact Dancho's bees at www.BizzBeeSolutions.com or reach out at Contact@BizzBeeSolutions.com